THE CAMBRIAN RAILWAYS
Volume I: 1852-1888

0—4—2 No 7 *Llanerchydol* leaves Abermule with a down local train in 1875, whilst 0—4—0ST No 36 *Plasfynnon* waits at the Kerry branch platform

THE
CAMBRIAN RAILWAYS

Volume I: 1852-1888

by

REX CHRISTIANSEN

&

R. W. MILLER

DAVID & CHARLES : NEWTON ABBOT

ISBN   0 7153 5236 9
First published in 1967
New edition 1971

BY THE SAME AUTHORS
The Cambrian Railways, Volume II: 1889-1968
The North Staffordshire Railway

Set in ten on eleven point Pilgrim
and printed in Great Britain
by W J Holman Limited Dawlish
for David & Charles (Publishers) Limited
South Devon House Newton Abbot Devon

Contents

Illustrations

RAILWAY COMPANIES' INITIALS PRINCIPALLY USED
IN THIS BOOK

Cambrian constituents

A & WC	Aberystwyth & Welsh Coast
L & N	Llanidloes & Newtown
MWR	Mid Wales Railway
N & M	Newtown & Machynlleth
O & N	Oswestry & Newtown
OE & W	Oswestry, Ellesmere & Whitchurch

Other railways

B & M	Brecon & Merthyr
CWR	Central Wales
GWR	Great Western
HH & B	Hereford, Hay & Brecon
LNWR	London & North Western
M & M	Manchester & Milford
N & B	Neath & Brecon
WMCQ	Wrexham, Mold & Connah's Quay

CEREMONY OF
Cutting the First Sod

Of the OSWESTRY SECTION of the
OSWESTRY, ELLESMERE, & WHITCHURCH
RAILWAY,
On Thursday, the 4th September, 1862,
AT OSWESTRY.

COMMITTEE OF MANAGEMENT:
CHAIRMAN—David Lloyd, Esq., Mayor of Oswestry.

Mr. Alderman Rogers	Mr. Councillor Dale	Mr. John Morris, builder
,, Alderman Morris	,, Councillor Saunders	,, David Rees, banker
,, Alderman Minshall	,, Councillor E. W. Thomas	Dr. Fuller
,, Councillor Phillips	,, Councillor John Thomas	Mr. I. F. Whitridge
,, Councillor Hilditch	,, Benjamin Roberts	,, Henry G. Weaver

TREASURER—Mr. Henry Davies. | HON. SEC.—Mr. Askew Roberts.

PROGRAMME:
THE DEMONSTRATION WILL BE COMMENCED AT 11 O'CLOCK IN THE MORNING, BY
A PROCESSION,
WHICH WILL
FORM ON THE BAILEY HEAD,
IN THE FOLLOWING ORDER:—

Brass Band.
King Oswald and Philanthropic Lodges of Odd-fellows.
Flags and Banners.
Band.
The Mayor and Corporation of Oswestry.
The Friends and Well-wishers.
The Railway Rifle Corps, headed by their Band.
The Directors, Officials, and Invited Guests.
Band.
The Court Duke of Cornwall Order of Foresters.
Flags and Banners.
The Ancient Briton Sun Friendly Society.
Drum and Fife Band.
The Juvenile Branch of Odd-fellows.
Flags and Banners.
The Children of the various Schools.
The Workmen.

The Friendly Societies will meet in the Horse Market, at Eleven o'clock, the Juvenile Lodge and the School-Children on the Bailey Head, and the Friends and Well-wishers in the Powis Hall, so as to be marshalled in proper order to accompany the Mayor and Corporation from the Council Chamber, as the clock strikes Twelve.

The Procession will march down Bailey Street, through the Cross, up Church Street, down Lower Brook Street, where it will turn off opposite the Dispensary, along Roft Street to the New Church, and up Salop Road to the Cross Keys, and thence through the New Road to the SHELF BANK FIELD, where

THE FIRST SOD WILL BE CUT
By Miss KINCHANT, of Park Hall.

The Barrow and Spade will be presented by Mr. SAVIN, the Contractor, and after the ceremony, a few complimentary speeches will be delivered from the Platform erected for the occasion.

At the conclusion of the Ceremony, the Procession will again form, with the Foresters and Sun Friendly Societies in front, the Odd-fellows bringing up the rear. In returning, the Procession will march up Beatrice Street and Albion Hill, to the Bailey Head, where it will separate. The Children will then be supplied with buns, &c., in the Powis Hall. At THREE o'clock,

A COLD COLLATION
WILL TAKE PLACE ON THE
WYNNSTAY ARMS BOWLING GREEN, IN A SPLENDID MARQUEE,
Erected for the occasion, and to which the Ladies are specially invited to attend, as well as Gentlemen.

After the Luncheon a select number of toasts will be proposed and responded to, after which the Tent will be cleared for a

RURAL FETE,
To which the Luncheon Tickets will admit. The Admission to those who have not attended the Luncheon will be One Shilling, by tickets, which may be purchased at the Bar of the Hotel.

Tickets for the Collation, 5s. each, may be had from Mr. Baugh, Ellesmere; at the Bar of the Wynnstay Arms Hotel, or from the *Advertiser* Office, Bailey Head, Oswestry.

The Committee hope that the persons composing the Procession will assist in keeping to the order of the Programme, both in going to, and returning from, the field, so as to prevent confusion.

☞ It is particularly requested that Ladies and Gentlemen intending to purchase tickets for the Collation, will do so on or before Monday, the 1st of September, that the Committee may have some idea how many guests they will have to provide for.

SPECIAL NOTICE.—The poorer women of the town and neighbourhood will be provided with Tea in the Tent on the Bowling Green, on Friday, the 5th September. Tickets may be had from any member of the Committee.

ASKEW ROBERTS, PRINTER, BAILEY HEAD, OSWESTRY.

Introduction

In some ways the Cambrian was a paradox. It was the largest of the independent Welsh companies—yet not the busiest. It stretched 300 miles through nine counties, yet never served a town bigger than Wrexham—and that as very much the junior of three companies. Everywhere it was hemmed in by other railways. In the north its traffic from the Lleyn Peninsula was siphoned off by the London & North Western *via* Carnarvon. What little lucrative traffic there was from Barmouth went mainly to the Great Western Railway *via* Dolgelley. The Manchester & Milford muscled in on traffic between Aberystwyth and West Wales, while the Mid Wales Railway never rose above being a rarely called-upon understudy to the Shrewsbury & Hereford. The Midland Railway further depleted what traffic was on offer from Swansea and Neath by routing it over its own line to Hereford.

Mainly, the Cambrian was something of a stopgap between the age of the horse and cart and the canal and the rural bus (which it helped to pioneer although not very successfully) and the motor car. Now, half a century later, even the rural bus is struggling for its life in mid-Wales. The motor car with the flexibility to go anywhere and everywhere at any time—all indispensable needs of country life—is omnipotent. It has come to stay forever while, at best, the Cambrian—now a shrunken part of the nationalised railway system, dieselised, Beeching-ised—can just about continue to hold its own. It will never again expand—and there is a danger that it will contract yet further.

The main line from Whitchurch to Machynlleth was built by four different companies which combined in 1864—less than ten years after their creation—to form The Cambrian Railways. (It may have been a comparatively small system, but it was always grandly plural!) A fifth company which built the line forward to Aberystwyth joined the consortium the following year and by 1869 the coast line to Pwllheli had been added, and also branches to Llanidloes, Porthywaen, Llanfyllin, Kerry and Dolgelley. Apart from the short branch to Nantmawr taken over in 1881, this was to remain the extent of the Cambrian system until the working of the Mid Wales Railway was taken over in 1888. This line of haunting beauty from Llanidloes to Talyllyn and thence to Brecon had a chequered independent career of its own.

This, then, is the period covered by the present volume. The second one develops the story from 1888 and tells of the construction of the later branches—to Wrexham, Llangynog, Llanfair Caereinion and Devil's Bridge. It tells of the creation—and struggles—of little independent lines: the Mawddwy Railway, the Van and the Elan Valley. There is the story of how the Cambrian grew up to become a main-line railway with daily expresses to London and Manchester (and many other towns in summer); of how, on Grouping with the GWR in 1922, it lost its identity, but not its atmosphere. Through Nationalisation, the story is brought forward to the present day.

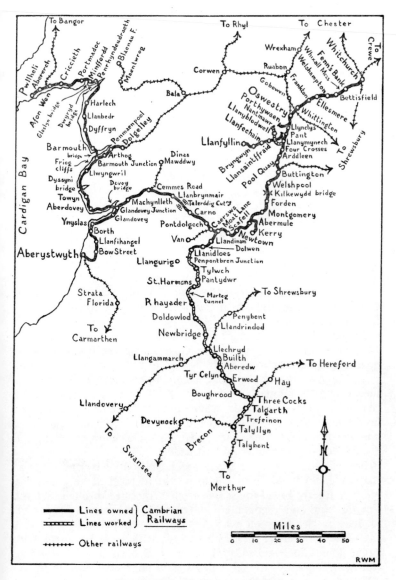

The Cambrian Railways in 1888

CHAPTER 1

The Prize beyond Reach

THROUGH MID-WALES TO IRELAND

Think first of a plan to drive a major railway through the deep valleys and under the barren mountains of central Wales to capture the rich traffic to and from America and Ireland.

Imagine now a modest, isolated single line of only twelve miles linking two small market towns. There you have the gulf between the dream and the reality of the early promoters in mid-Wales. Railways arrived late in the area but, once they got a foothold, they spread like fire through a tinder-dry forest. As the planners got to work it seemed as if every valley which could possibly accommodate a line (and several which could not) was ready to welcome the arrival of the steam train.

The first body to consider railways in mid-Wales was the Irish Railway Commission, which the Government set up in 1836 to investigate the best route to Ireland. The following year it asked C. B. Vignoles, one of the most prominent engineers of the day, to survey a route from Shrewsbury to Porth Dinlleyn on the north coast of the Lleyn Peninsula, where a major harbour was envisaged inside the wide, sandy and sheltered bay. Coming from England, his line was planned through Llangollen, Bala, Dolgelley and along the coast through Barmouth and Portmadoc.

Brunel, who was also actively seeking a London-Ireland route at that time, favoured Porth Dinlleyn, but to reach it he planned a more southerly broad-gauge line from Worcester through Ludlow, Craven Arms and Montgomery and over the Severn on a 170 ft high viaduct at Newtown. It was then to run up Talerddig to Dinas Mawddwy and under Cader Idris to reach the coast. If this broad-gauge main line, laid out for speed, had been built, the whole railway geography of mid-Wales would have evolved differently. All other lines would have been subsidiary to it and the Cambrian system would never have been built in anything like its eventual form.

But Brunel was defeated by the initiative of the Chester & Crewe Railway, which asked George Stephenson to survey a route along the coastal strip between Chester and Holyhead, while reporting on the Porth Dinlleyn alternative. In his mind there was only one possible route. The Porth Dinlleyn line, he reported in 1839, would be 'prefectly impracticable in the general acceptation of the term as regards railways'. It would involve a 10-mile climb at 1 in 150 to a summit of 590 ft—while the Holyhead line would be almost level for 70 miles. Tunnels and excavations needed to reach Porth Dinlleyn would be greater than any so far attempted and the whole project was most unfit for either a private company or the Government to carry out. The only good point he could find about the plan was that it would avoid a crossing of the Menai Strait.

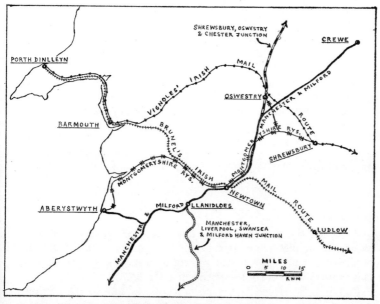

Some proposed railways 1837-55

The Railway Commissioners liked Brunel's scheme, although they admitted the coast line had many advantages, especially when it was preferred by the Admiralty which claimed that Porth Dinlleyn was liable to silt up. But even their Lordships' firm pronouncement did not quite settle the issue.

When no start had been made on building the Holyhead line by the summer of 1843, Brunel asked Vignoles to make a more detailed survey of his broad-gauge route, but only a few months later the London & Birmingham and Grand Junction Railways were forced to take action to meet the threat of GWR competition for Irish traffic through South Wales. After the Chester & Holyhead was incorporated on 4 July 1844, Porth Dinlleyn was doomed as a cross-channel port.

A fresh attempt to drive a main line from Worcester was made during the 1846 Railway Mania, which also threw up a suggestion for a Welsh Midland Railway from Worcester to Brecon via Hereford and Hay. About the same time the North Wales & Dublin Railway & Harbour Company was projected to build a branch to Porth Dinlleyn from the Chester & Holyhead at Bangor 'to secure an efficient line of communication with Ireland'. Capital was to be £700,000, but the scheme never got off the ground.

A better-remembered plan launched at this time was that of the Manchester & Milford Railway, which ambitiously aimed at making Milford a rival port to Liverpool for American cotton. Its planners were undeterred by Milford having been in decline as a port since the removal of the Royal Dockyard in 1811. They wanted to forward traffic by rail via Carmarthen, Lampeter, Llanidloes, Newtown, Oswestry, Whitchurch and Crewe. A traffic balance was to be maintained by goods sent from Lancashire for export. This grand scheme was dropped almost as soon as it was born in 1845—no doubt to the chagrin of the directors, 86 in number!

CANALS AND TRAMROADS

Although the Railway Mania failed to develop any lines in mid-Wales, its echoes were strong enough to make canal owners band together to offset the threat of competition and, in 1845, several canals merged to form the Shropshire Union.

Canals had arrived in the Border country late in the eighteenth century and they included two of the SU constituents—the Ellesmere and Montgomeryshire systems, which had been authorised in 1793 and 1794 to open up the area. The Ellesmere Canal was planned to run from Shrewsbury, via Ruabon and Chester, to the Mersey at what is now Ellesmere Port. It was designed with several branches, including Frankton to Ellesmere, Prees and Whitchurch, and Frankton to Llanymynech. The section from Chester to Ellesmere Port was opened first in 1795. It was followed two years later

ALONG THE COAST

(1) *Under the crags of Harlech Castle—'Beaconsfield' 4—4—0 No. 50
with the 2.43 p.m. up from Pwllheli on 15 July 1911*

(2) *Rebuilt 0—6—0 No. 10 lumbers along between Harlech and
Llanbedr on an up goods on 25 July 1911*

EXPRESS PASSENGER

(3) *Rebuilt 4—4—0 No. 17 on the 12.31 p.m. through express from Pwllheli nearing Dovey Junction on 17 July 1912*

(4) *Aston 4—4—0 No. 64 climbing Talerddig bank*

by the Llanymynech branch and the connecting part of the main line as far as Chirk Bank. By 1801 the main line extended to Vron and Weston and the Ellesmere, Prees and Whitchurch branches were open. In 1805 the short extension from Vron to Plas Kynaston (Cefn) was opened together with a new line from Whitchurch to the Chester Canal at Hurleston. The rest of the main line, from Cefn to Chester and from Weston to Shrewsbury, was never built. The last part of the Ellesmere Canal to open was that through Llangollen to Llantysilio in 1808. Thus the Ellesmere Canal was split into two sections joined only by the Chester Canal (Chester to Nantwich). The Ellesmere and Chester Canals amalgamated in 1813.

The Ellesmere and Montgomeryshire Canals met end-on at Carreghofa, near Llanymynech, and the 'eastern' branch of the Montgomeryshire was planned from Porthywaen lime rocks to Welshpool and Garthmyl, near Montgomery. It was opened in 1797, followed later by the short Guildsfield branch from Burgeddin to Tyddyn, but powers to extend up the Severn Valley to Newtown with what became the 'western' branch were not sought until 1815. They were received a few days after Waterloo and the branch was completed in 1821. This was as far as canals penetrated in the Border country, although there were subsequent proposals to extend the Shropshire Union from Newtown to Llanidloes as an alternative to a railway. Canals always suffered from severe limitations in the hilly terrain and the superiority of railways was quickly seen, but the canal owners showed foresight in getting and exploiting powers to build small feeder lines.

A number of these were built along the Border and the most southerly was the Welsh Pool Rail Road, which ran three-quarters of a mile from the Stondart Quarries to the canal, probably from 1818. It was the world's first railway to fit rails into chairs, and although it fell into disuse by 1854, part of its route was later adapted by the Welshpool & Llanfair Light Railway.

Further north, two short lines ran from Llanymynech Hill, a rich limestone area. One served lime kilns beside the canal until 1914. The other, which terminated near a spot where the Cambrian later planned to bridge the canal, closed in 1899. Pant station was built over another line from hillside quarries.

A 2 ft 6 in. gauge tramway, opened from Crickheath Wharf to Llynclys in 1820, was extended about six years later to Porthywaen Limestone Quarry. The line, which used wagons built to carry four tons of stone, was in use until 1913. All these canal feeders were built under the aegis of the Earl of Powis, whose family was

B

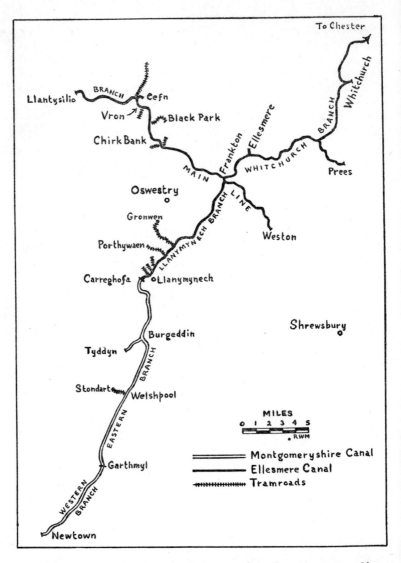

Canals and associated tramroads. More were planned: a company at Llanymynech deposited a Bill on 23 December 1858 to build a branch and tramways
to the Lime Rocks from the Oswestry & Newtown Railway, which was to
have powers to operate both systems.

destined to play a major role in Cambrian railway history.

Meanwhile, three small coal-pits at Morda, south of Oswestry, got the canal company's approval to build a tramway linking them to a wharf called Gronwen after one of the pits. Laid down to a gauge of 3 ft 1 in., the line had primitive cast-iron rails of only 4 ft 6 in. in length and stone sleepers, but it survived until about 1879.

The only role of the feeder lines—and there were others to the canal north of Frankton—was to carry minerals. But even so, they were invaluable in speeding up traffic in the heyday of the horse wagon.

The concept of feeder tramroads from mines and quarries to local ports was exploited all round the coast of Wales and it was also the 1812 birthright of the Hay Railway and later the Festiniog, the Croesor, the Corris, Machynlleth and River Dovey Tramroads, the Gorsedda Junction & Portmadoc Railway and the Talyllyn.

Canals greatly helped in the speed-up of trade. Before they arrived in the Border Country, it took horse teams four days to get two tons of coal or lime into country districts.

After they merged together, the canals set about planning their own railway to take them into the steam age and, in 1846, the Shropshire Union Railway & Canal Company got powers for several projects, including a line from Newtown to Crewe along a route which would have involved converting part of the canal. By this move, the canal showed itself ready to pass its own death sentence. Yet at the same time, the tactic was political, aimed at getting good terms for leasing the canal to the LNWR, which was then actively seeking a conquest into mid-Wales.

Also in 1846, the LNW's rival—the Shrewsbury, Oswestry & Chester Junction Railway—got powers for a branch from Gobowen, through Oswestry, to the SU's proposed route at Crickheath, near Llanymynech. Soon afterwards, the SO & CJ merged with the North Wales Mineral Railway to form the Shrewsbury & Chester. Plans changed the following year when the LNWR leased the SU and dropped the Newtown-Crewe scheme. As a result, the S & C cut back its single line from Gobowen to Oswestry and the line, of just under three miles, was opened on 23 December 1848.

Now, with the railways' first tiny foothold established in mid-Wales, it is time to review the strategic position throughout the whole of Wales. The most important development had been the opening of the Holyhead line by the LNWR. In the south, the GWR had reached Swansea and was driving west. Along the Border, the

Shrewsbury-Hereford route was about to be constructed and both companies were looking for a springboard to prevent the other's entry into mid-Wales. Commercial and industrial life in the Border Country moved slowly in these early Victorian years of deep peace, and the arrival of the railway in such a key town as Oswestry brought no immediate agitation for its extension.

Finally, in 1852, a new scheme emerged. Under the title of the Montgomeryshire Railways Company, a line was proposed from Shrewsbury through Minsterley (rather than Welshpool), Newtown, Llanidloes and Llangurig to Aberystwyth, with a branch to Oswestry from Garthmyl. The LNWR adopted the plan, but amended the route through Criggion (junction for a branch to Oswestry), Welshpool and Machynlleth, thus avoiding Llanidloes. The western part of this scheme was eventually dropped before it went before Parliament.

DEFEAT OF THE GIANTS

The people of Llanidloes were furious and they reacted quickly with a plan of their own. They had already shown that they were not a community to be trifled with when they got fed up with the way the town was being run in 1839. They remedied that grievance by taking over the town and running it themselves for three days until troops had to be called in. And they had to stay to garrison the town for several months until tempers calmed down. Now, the fact that the LNWR—an English company—had administered the snub probably added relish to the townspeople's determination to get a railway. So they planned to build a line themselves to link up with the Montgomeryshire Railways at Newtown.

Llanidloes and Newtown were both boroughs which had developed round the manufacturing industries rather than as farming centres, the change of emphasis in the economy having taken place with the extension of the canal to Newtown. It shared, with Welshpool, the administration of the County of Montgomery. One of the most prominent leaders was William Pugh of Kerry. He was a magistrate and road builder. He was interested in railways from their earliest days and had backed the first efforts to get them into mid-Wales.

Llanidloes was also a prosperous, and bigger, flannel town with a medieval flannel market that is still a prominent feature of the town centre. Its population in the 1850s was over 4,500—compared with under 4,000 in Newtown. The scheme to join the two towns by rail had many advantages. The promoters held their first meeting at

Llanidloes on 30 October 1852 under the chairmanship of George Hammond Whalley, a magistrate for the three surrounding counties and a dominating, thrusting, impulsive and explosive Irishman, who was also, for a time, Member of Parliament for Peterborough.

A prospectus was approved which sought support for the line not only locally, but in Aberystwyth and any other town likely to be interested. It estimated that a capital of £60,000 would be needed. Annual receipts, estimated at £8,250, were expected to yield a dividend of 7 per cent. The first subscriptions were sufficient to prepare a Parliamentary Bill and the route was surveyed by Rice Hopkins, whose father had laid the Penydarran Tramway from Dowlais to Abercynon, the first line in the world to use a locomotive.

Preparation of the Bill meant that, in the 1853 Parliamentary session, three schemes were arraigned before Members. The Commons threw out the Shrewsbury & Chester's Newtown extension plans and that for the Montgomeryshire Railways, but accepted the Llanidloes & Newtown scheme—the most modest. But the Lords dismissed it when they found Hopkins' levels were false: at one point they showed the line running 18 ft below the Severn! The 12¼-mile route was quickly revised to show it falling from 535 ft above sea level at Llanidloes to 312 ft at Scafell and, after crossing the Severn, climbing to 399 ft at a proposed junction with the Aberystwyth line at Newtown. The steepest gradient was a short length at 1 in 120. The main obstacle was the river, which was to be crossed no less than four times by timber trestle bridges.

THE LLANIDLOES & NEWTOWN RAILWAY

The revised Bill went through Parliament and the Llanidloes & Newtown Railway was incorporated on 4 August 1853. It promptly celebrated by proposing its own extensions to Oswestry and Shrewsbury. The mid-Wales railway revolution had exploded from within, but it nearly fizzled out through lack of money. The L & N could not at first raise enough money to start its authorised line, let alone pay for extensions. The L & N board was formed in October with Whalley as chairman and seven other directors.

The L & N's expansion ideas were taken out of its hands by the formation of another company—the Oswestry & Newtown, again with Whalley at the helm. The O & N got its Act on 26 June 1855 —before work had started on the L & N, which was still engaged in a long struggle to raise funds. Tenders to build the L & N were finally invited on 28 September 1855 and they were returnable by a stated hour—7 o'clock in the evening of the fourth day. They stipulated that cash would be paid monthly. Of seven tenders for the first two miles from Llanidloes to Morfedian, the lowest came from a local contractor: David Davies (1818-90), who lived at Llandinam beside the route. For Davies, it was another job in a career which was to make him one of the ablest and greatest self-made men of Wales in the nineteenth century. Although he is often remembered for his work on the Cambrian (including 77 miles of the constituents) and other Welsh railways, his finest achievements were in coal mining. But they lay in the future and we move on to preparations which he made for the more humble job of constructing two miles of line. It was at a time when local landowners were being urged, because of the benefit which they would receive from the railway, to take up shares and charge rent for land, rather than ask for purchase. The aim was to reduce the amount of capital needed to get work under way.

Although this was a pioneer railway, not everyone behind it pulled together. Victorian protocol was at its height—as the board found out when they asked one of the main shareholders, Mrs Ann Owen of Glansevern, to cut the first sod. A local newspaper gave the news that she was to carry out the ceremony on the site of Llanidloes station on 3 October, before she had accepted the invitation. She was furious and retorted by advertising, without telling the directors, that the ceremony was being postponed. But having nursed the infant plan so far, the directors were not to be put off by a clash of personalities and the ceremony went ahead on time with the chairman cutting the first sod in pouring rain. Cannons were fired, church bells rung and 5,000 people marched in a celebration procession a quarter of a mile long.

The original plan was for a double line but this was amended to single, although bridges were built to allow for a second line being laid with a minimum of trouble and expense. It was a decision which set the pattern for the development of all the mid-Wales lines.

A month after work began, Davies got the contract for the second section and, eventually, the whole line, but by then he had taken into partnership Thomas Savin (1826-89) of Llwyn-y-Maen. Savin was another figure who was to dominate the Welsh railway scene at different times, often in a flamboyant way, and his driving power was felt when schemes slowed down. Yet he never achieved the eminence of David Davies.

Up to 600 navvies shaped the modest earthworks and laid the track but progress was slow, even allowing for the difficulties of getting materials to an area thirty miles from the nearest railway. It meant a tedious haul by canal and rough roads for most of the materials needed.

Yet the start of work was sufficient to provide the impetus for a third stage of development in mid-Wales. It came with the crystallising of plans for a line from the L & N at Caersws across the mountains which lay between the Upper Severn Valley and the sea, to Machynlleth. A survey was completed and a prospectus issued before the end of 1856 and it led to the formation of the Newtown & Machynlleth Railway on 27 July 1857.

To pick up the story of the L & N, Llandinam was reached in August 1856 and three-quarters of the line—as far as Penstrowed—was ready by the end of the next year. Then funds ran out and work stopped. Shareholders readily agreed to the contractor's suggestion to lease the line, but no work was done during 1858 and Davies and Savin went off to build the 10-mile Vale of Clwyd Railway between Rhyl and Denbigh. They received part payment in shares and worked the line for a year and this seemed the obvious solution for the desperate L & N. Early in 1859, Davies and Savin offered to finish it for all unissued shares and debentures (representing a 25 per cent rise on the original contract), and to work the line. Despite opposition from the chairman, a committee of shareholders recommended acceptance and the lease was incorporated into the 1859 L & N (Canal Extension) Act. The extension was to be a tramway running a quarter of a mile from the main line to the SU canal basin at Newtown. It was not built because of the high cost of yet another crossing of the Severn and also because work had restarted on the Oswestry & Newtown, which would make the canal connection unnecessary. The Act was dated 21 July 1859.

The construction of the L & N was resumed with the excavation of Scafell cutting, with the work in charge of Benjamin Piercy (1827-88) of Trefeglwys, another local man, who had become engineer in 1858 after the death of Rice Hopkins. Piercy had assisted Henry Robertson on the Shrewsbury & Chester and was associated with Davies and Savin on the Vale of Clwyd.

The line was quickly finished to a temporary terminus at Newtown and a service of goods trains started on 30 April 1859, although it was not until 9 August that the Board of Trade issued a passenger certificate. The official opening, by a now placated Mrs Owen, took place on 31 August.

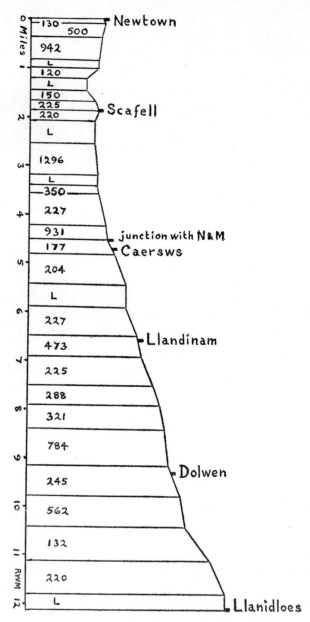

Gradient profile: Llanidloes & Newtown Railway

The next day—before the start of regular trains—was one of celebration as Davies and Savin gave a 'grand festal entertainment' to friends and the 600 navvies at Llandinam—Davies' native village. A large arch was built across the line and the *Llanidloes & Newtown Telegraph* reported:

> From an early hour this village was the seen (*sic*) of mirth and jollity. The bells of the venerable church rang spirited peals, while cannon placed on the adjacent hills fired salutes at intervals during the day.

Celebrations began with a parade through Newtown to the station to join a special train which only arrived 'after a wait of some time'. It ran through to Llanidloes before returning to Llandinam for the feast at which one of the speakers saw the L & N as

> a railway which will form a link of a line eventually destined to pierce through the centre of Wales, to open her picturesque valleys to the tourist, to enable the miner to work profitably the minerals with which she abounds, and to render her barren soils fertile by the facility with which the farmer can obtain the lime so necessary to those soils.

The next day was not such a cheerful one for Whalley for he went to Rhayader to preside at the cutting of the first sod of the Mid Wales Railway—a ceremony which was to end in a storm.

From the start of the regular L & N trains on 2 September—the first in mid-Wales—they called at Dolwen, Llandinam and Caersws. There was no crossing place and stations were simple, single platforms. As there was no telegraph, the timetable had to be strictly enforced to avoid two trains being on the line at once.

Although four locomotives were ordered from Sharp Stewart & Company of Manchester to work the line, other engines were used in its construction. The first *Dove* reached Llandinam in 1857 *via* the Oswestry railhead. From there it was carried on a special wagon, built by Davies and pulled by 14 horses. Davies, a staunch Methodist, refused to allow any movement on a Sunday and *Dove* became the centre of great interest as the first locomotive seen in Montgomeryshire when it stood by the roadside on a Sunday. It was followed by *Squirrel*, *Llewellyn* and *Enterprise*.

Until the completion of the line to Oswestry on 10 June 1861, the L & N remained isolated and all stores were carried by canal to Newtown and carted across the town to the station.

Although the L & N was physically isolated for so long, the directors continually pressed for a link with South Wales and announced plans for a link through a 10 mile line between Llanidloes and Llandovery. They felt confident enough of success to state in *Brad-*

shaw's Railway Manual for 1859 :

> With the exception of a tunnel three-quarters of a mile in extent at
> the Llandovery end, the works will be comparatively light, and the
> line made for £7,000 a mile. This link supplied, the communication
> between Manchester and Milford will be complete.

The directors went on to say :

> It is now ascertained that the Cardiganshire route does not present the
> engineering and commercial difficulties which have been so much
> spoken of, and that a line at a gradient of 1 in 80 will be able to reach
> Cwmystwith and the Hafod Valley with less than one and a half mile
> of tunnelling.

From 3 January 1863 the L & N's status changed again when it
became in effect a branch of the main line when it was opened
through from Machynlleth to Oswestry. Caersws station was closed
and replaced by one nearer Newtown at the junction at Moat Lane.
Bradshaw had named Moat Lane station from the opening of the
line, but Murray's *Handbook for Travellers in North Wales* (1861)
which deals with individual stations only mentions Caersws. An
extra station was opened at Scafell about the same time. Early in
1864 the through station built at Llanidloes in readiness for the opening of the Mid Wales Railway to Brecon was completed and the
L & N, as joint owner, changed stations and closed its old terminus.

The main line from Whitchurch to Aberystwyth was opened
throughout on 27 July 1864. Two days earlier, the L & N had ceased
to exist as an independent company when it amalgamated together
with three more of the five railways forming the main line—the
Oswestry & Newtown, Newtown & Machynlleth and the Oswestry,
Ellesmere & Whitchurch—to form the Cambrian Railways. A fifth
line, the Aberystwyth & Welsh Coast Railway, joined the
consortium just over a year later.

CHAPTER 2

Relief from Isolation

THE OSWESTRY & NEWTOWN RAILWAY

None of the thirty miles of the Oswestry & Newtown Railway was anywhere near completion when the Llanidloes & Newtown was opened. But the position soon changed when Davies and Savin, who were looking round for work after completing the L & N, took over the contract from one who had gone bankrupt.

But that is jumping ahead of events. To get the position in perspective we must look back at some of the events which took place parallel with the L & N's sluggish development. The promoters of the O & N signed an agreement with the contracting firm of Thornton & McCormick on 11 January 1855—six months ahead of the Act of 26 June, which termed the company the Oswestry, Welchpool (with a 'c' as was common at that time) & Newtown Railway, although subsequently, it is interesting to note, there were few references made to the middle town in connection with the company's title.

The Oswestry & Newtown was only able to rescue the L & N from isolation after its own birth had been long and difficult. The English giants were still smarting at being out-manoeuvred during the creation of the L & N and they were opposed to any extension of it independent of either of them. And both were in stronger positions than they had been when the L & N was incorporated. The GWR held a much tighter grip on the Border because of its absorption of the Shrewsbury & Chester Railway on 1 September 1854. It now set out to get control of a line from Oswestry to Newtown. Its early moves met with some success for, at the inaugural meeting of the O & N, it forced the promoters to drop the idea of a branch running from Welshpool to Shrewsbury and thus joining the LNWR. But it turned out to be a Pyrrhic victory, for some of the O & N promoters were in close sympathy with the LNWR and ready to fight for a Shrewsbury link. The group, which included the Earl of Powis, the largest landowner concerned, broke away and presented a separate Bill.

Yet after they did so in 1856, the GWR did not lose its strong influence on the O & N board and it had four directors until 1859.

The route of the O & N lay along the Border through a string of small towns and villages, the most important of which was Welshpool. This borough had been built a mile away from the Severn to avoid severe floods which often covered the low-lying valley. By this time Welshpool, though still growing slowly in size and commercial importance, had lost its status as the biggest flannel-making town in Montgomeryshire. Welshpool now had a population of 6,000, but Newtown and Llanidloes were now larger centres of the flannel trade. The railway by-passed by nearly two miles the county town itself, where there had been much support for its construction. But the reasons were valid: the ancient walled town built on a hill was little bigger than a village. Its population was under 500 and it was not an important centre of trade as most county towns were. The only other intermediate town of any size was Llanymynech, the centre of several lime quarries and kilns, with about 1,000 people. Oswestry was the dominating town with a population of 9,000 and industries which included tanning and malting.

It was natural that, with its pro-GWR complexion, the O & N Bill should be opposed by the LNWR, but it did not even succeed in getting a hearing in the Lords. The capital of £250,000 was backed by loans of £83,000 and eventually it had a capital of £730,000.

It soon ran into the sort of troubles which had bedevilled the L & N. They began when the contractors were unable to start work. After the winter of 1855-6 shareholders appointed a committee to investigate. It went about the job leisurely and did not report to the directors until 27 June 1857—two years and one day after the passing of the Act. Its findings were straightforward: it recommended that new contractors should be appointed and, to reduce costs, that earthworks should be built for a single line only. In every other work the route was to be prepared for doubling.

The solicitor, Abraham Howell of Welshpool (1810-93), put before the board a draft letter to Thornton & McCormick which stated that, because of insuperable obstacles, the O & N felt morally as well as legally justified in refusing to continue negotiations for completion of the line as they would only prove futile. Not every director agreed: some felt the board should detail the difficulties, but Thornton & McCormick were dismissed and on 10 July the Piercy Brothers, who were now resident engineers, reported that another firm—Davidson & Oughterson—was prepared to build a single line, doubled at Oswestry, Welshpool and Newtown, for

£206,400. It would also maintain the line for a year after opening
and take a fifth of the bill in shares.

Joseph Cubitt, the O & N's engineer from inception, recommended
that a start should be made on the 6½ miles south from Oswestry
as this would include the biggest task—the Llanymynech rock
cutting. This was estimated to account for £48,000 of the £112,000
for the Oswestry-Welshpool section. It also involved bridging
several tramways near Llanymynech because the Act stipulated

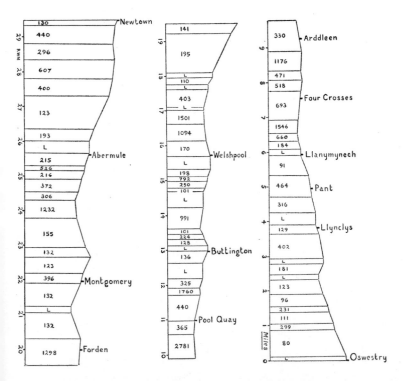

Gradient profile: Oswestry & Newtown Railway

that the line must not interfere with them by crossing them on the
level. Cubitt was also anxious to start immediate work on other
sections and, when money ran short, he pleaded for work to be
authorised on the Severn bridges at Buttington and near Pool Quay.
This was to take advantage of the river level while it was low in
summer for the laying of bridge foundations. The first sod was cut

by the bowling green at Welshpool on 4 August—a day later than first announced—by Lady Watkin Williams-Wynn and the ceremony was surrounded by the usual elaborate ritual with the thunder being stolen by guns, captured by Clive in India, which were fired from Powis Castle.

Long negotiations began about a joint station at Oswestry. The GWR wanted it as near as possible to its Gobowen branch terminus so as to avoid building fresh approaches from the town. When the Town Council stated that it would prefer a station at Cross Keys, the GWR replied firmly that it had no money to build an approach and the Council would have to bear the cost. Once the site was agreed close to the GWR station, agreements followed between the O & N and other companies. On 14 August 1860 the GWR got running powers and authority to have its own booking clerks and porters, provided they handled only the company's traffic. On 30 January 1861 the O & N agreed to access for the Oswestry, Ellesmere & Whitchurch and also the LNWR if it wanted it.

Meanwhile, the O & N was struggling to sort out its own problems. Apart from a continual shortage of money, work was often held up by difficulties in getting land. Mrs Ann Owen, who had already shown how forthright she could be, refused to have the O & N near her home 'Glansevern', near Berriew (even though she was a shareholder), and it had to be diverted to the opposite bank of the river, which meant building a two-mile bank at 1 in 110/195 up to Forden. The steepest gradient of 1 in 80 was in the final stretch of the 2¼-mile bank up to Oswestry from the south.

RESCUE BY DAVIES AND SAVIN

By February 1858, land difficulties near Oswestry were so serious that less than three miles of line were ready. Then Davidson & Oughterson went bankrupt with only 11 of the 30 miles started —and far from complete. The O & N was at a standstill and the LNWR was quick to see the situation as an opportunity to break through across the Border to Newtown. The plan was to convert the Shropshire Union Canal into an extension of the Shrewsbury-Welshpool line. It was a threat which could have meant the virtual death of the O & N with shareholders losing their capital. But the LNWR and SU did not turn threat into action and the crisis passed when Davies and Savin took over the O & N contract. They found the O & N heavily in debt, but the take-over was the turning point, as C. S. Denniss (the Cambrian's general manager) pointed out in an interview in the *Railway Magazine* in 1903. He described it as 'a change and success far exceeding all expectations and remarkable even in the history of railways'.

Lawsuits—which Denniss described as 'gigantic'—abounded. The O & N's second chairman, Sir Watkin Williams-Wynn, was being sued for £75,000, and Davies and Savin paid off £45,000 to get work on the line restarted. They agreed to complete it in exchange for unissued preference shares and debentures and earnings up to 1 January 1861. Two directors—Lord Powis and Richard Mytton—resigned in protest against this method of finance. This could have been a blow to the O & N's fortunes as the influence of the Powis family was strong: the Act of Incorporation gave the owner of Powis Castle power to appoint a director.

But all was well. About this time, the Shrewsbury & Welshpool Railway suggested that the stretch between Buttington and Welshpool should be double-track. The O & N were negotiating traffic arrangements with the LNWR and, to maintain good relations, the O & N agreed to the doubling. This became the first work carried out by Davies and Savin and they started on it on 30 October 1859.

Once it became clear to the LNWR that the O & N was back on a firm footing, it withdrew its canal conversion threat in January 1860 and instead accepted running powers to Welshpool and O & N support for several bills which it had pending. It paid £25,000 for access to Welshpool and asked for the Buttington doubling to be completed by 1 January 1861, or sooner if needed. Under an agreement of 30 January 1861 the LNWR paid half the maintenance costs on Welshpool station, where passenger expenses were shared and goods paid in proportion. It was an agreement which was to lead to lengthy wrangling.

The contract with Davies and Savin put real heart into the O & N and on the eve of work restarting it prepared a Bill not only allowing it to continue arrangements with them, but also to build a branch from Llynclys to serve quarries at Porthywaen; to amalgamate or make working arrangements with neighbouring companies, and to raise capital with them towards linking the Montgomeryshire railways with South Wales.

The Bill was passed on 3 July 1860. The first sixteen miles from Oswestry to Pool Quay had been open since 1 May, and the section to Welshpool followed on 14 August—the same day as the opening of an isolated five-mile stretch from Abermule to Newtown, where a joint station with the L & N had been agreed eleven months earlier.

Soon afterwards there came further delays because of a row,

involving companies as well as contractors, over plans to reach the coast of Cardigan Bay. David Howell (a Machynlleth solicitor and younger brother of Abraham) planned a line from there to Aberystwyth passing near Borth and it was to join a line which the Corris Railway was considering extending along the coast to Towyn. While Davies and most of the directors of the Newtown & Machynlleth Railway lined up behind Howell's scheme, Savin envisaged a more ambitious system of railways stretching along the whole coast to Porth Dinlleyn. The scheme was to include the development of a 'string of watering places' and big hotels at Aberystwyth, Borth and Aberdovey. To fill them, Savin planned to offer combined rail and hotel tickets. This 'think big' scheme also had the powerful support of the Oswestry & Newtown and the Llanidloes & Newtown, which saw it as the source of greatly-increased through traffic and they offered to subscribe £100,000—three-quarters coming from the O & N.

Davies and his main supporter Thomas Webb (then his secretary and later chairman of Davies' Ocean Coal Company and a director of the Barry Railway & Docks) rested their case on the slow progress which was then being made on building the Newtown & Machynlleth. They regarded Savin as reckless and his coast scheme as 'hairbrained'. The rift was so deep that Davies dissolved their partnership on 29 October 1860. The bitterness lingered in letters written to the *Railway Times*, with Savin alleging that Davies had poached Webb away from him. So broke up another of the uneasy marriages of temperament which were common among Welsh railway promoters in the early years. While Savin was gambling his way along a road which was to reduce him to bankruptcy, Davies continued to exercise the restraint and caution with which he was to make his permanent mark in mining, as well as in railway building. But it was also an attitude which was to lead to a tempestuous row and petty spite against the Cambrian. But that lay in the years ahead. As we shall see later, the split had its impact on the building of the Newtown & Machynlleth, on which the men were engaged at the same time. Meanwhile, Savin carried on alone the working of the Oswestry and Llanidloes companies. Through running between both towns started with the completion of the nine-mile gap between Abermule and Welshpool on 10 June 1861. Under a 21-year agreement from 26 July, Savin provided the stock and took 55 per cent of the gross receipts.

Even this step forward did not put an end to enmity as was demonstrated in a letter which someone calling himself *Justitia*

THE ORIGINAL BARMOUTH BRIDGE IN 1898

(5) *Rebuilt 2—4—0 No. 54 coasts off the bridge and round the curves towards Barmouth with a northbound train*

(6) *The same engine returns with an up train and crosses the drawbridge*

CONSTRUCTION AND DESTRUCTION

(7) *David Davies supervising work on constructing Talerddig Cutting :
the top-hatted figure on the gantry spanning the cutting in which
gold was found*

(8) *'Pegasus' lying smashed on Friog Rocks after the 1883 avalanche*

wrote to a local paper from Montgomery. Dated 25 August (1861), it read:

'A Shareholder' has appeared in a great public capacity, seizing every newspaper, and also issuing a most magniloquent pamphlet, repudiating and denouncing the Oswestry and Newtown Board of Directors. It is all no doubt very proper, and possibly the shareholder may not be the same as the 'pamphleteer', but may have a double: still that is of no consequence.

The figures of the 'Shareholder' are very elaborate, but they can have nothing to do with the Company's affairs.

The so-called 'flourish of trumpets' on the West Midland question did not come to grief through want of the West Midland and the Great Western trying, by every available means, to carry it out; but simply through those two companies having made another agreement to swallow the unfortunate 'Shareholder' and all others.

To this the Oswestry and Newtown Directors were awake, and consequently were enabled to foil the dirty dodge.

I will only say one word about Mr Whalley, the chairman. He has been abused, because he was nobody—he is now abused because he is everybody; his name was dragged before the House of Commons in the most disgraceful manner by the Great Western Company, who ought to have been ashamed of their conduct, and now that he has put himself in a prominent position in Montgomeryshire, of which I presume he is proud, the satellites of that Company still abuse him.

I have no further space to enter into the letter, but have a few words to say about the pamphlet.

The pamphlet alludes to the ornaments of the Board, the great names in Montgomeryshire who were once Directors! Why did they retire when they had all in their own hands—with a glorious share list and, I admit, immense aristocratic support? They had, also, unbounded control over the Board. All these immense resources failed, the money was squandered, the Company was apparently ruined, and the solicitor recommended the works to be stopped.

Under these circumstances, two only of the Directors stood true to the ship. The day of trial came, three Directors only met, one tried to stop all proceedings, and demanded his expenses—our late respected Chairman gave way to the urgent entreaty of Mr Piercy, and the Company was saved from ruin.

Such is the history of this unfortunate Company up to that date.

When Messrs Davies and Savin agreed to take up the thing, Lord Powis expressed himself in strong terms as to their liberality, Sir Watkin was highly delighted; all in fact were pleased.

Well, the Contractors have carried out these terms. Mr Davies has, fortunately for the Company, retired, and Mr Savin has conceded a point by giving up the lease, which will be of enormous advantage to the shareholders.

I believe the great shareholders named in the pamphlet—Lord Powis, Mr Naylor and Mrs Owen—will use every exertion to back the efforts of the Board in trying to retrieve a once ruined affair.

As regards the Investigation Committee, I believe it was a farce.

C

Further, as to the remarks in the pamphlet about figures, we may safely leave them to the shareholders.

One other thing I will refer to—Mr D. Davies's letter. He has now in his employment Mr Savin's late private secretary, and that may probably account for that letter.

In conclusion I will only state, that when the present Board took up the management, the shares were worth £15 per 100 all calls paid; they are now worth more than £80, 12 per cent more than the Great Western, and the victimised shareholder had better dispose of his small shares to prevent ruin.

The split between the men was not the only cause of delay in completing the O & N. Extra time needed to divert the line around Mrs Owen's estate and to complete Kilkewydd bridge built on the skew over the Severn, also contributed to it. The bridge was finished on 27 May when the locomotive *Leighton* safely crossed and the whole line was passed by the Board of Trade the following week. The only other large bridge on the O & N not yet mentioned spanned the Vyrnwy at Llanymynech. Crossing loops were provided at most of the intermediate stations: Llynclys, Llanymynech, Welshpool, Montgomery and Abermule. Single platform stations without loops were at Four Crosses, Pool Quay and Forden.

The opening of the line to Shrewsbury in 1862 was coupled with a new station at Cefn (soon renamed Buttington) and the double section to Welshpool was brought into use at the same time. Extra stations were established at Pant and Arddleen by 1864, but they were without loops.

The first headquarters of the O & N were in temporary offices opened at Oswestry in July 1859. They moved to Welshpool the following February and were established in the station, which had been built to house them. When the move was made Constable Patrick Charles Fegan, who had looked after the offices at Oswestry, was sacked, but when he died a few months later the company gave £5 towards funeral expenses. The O & N's stay at Welshpool was also short for it decided on 26 September 1861 that it was necessary to have its headquarters in London. The move was made the following January together with other companies, the object being to facilitate the mass of Parliamentary committee work.

With the L & N, Oswestry, Ellesmere & Whitchurch, Wrexham, Mold & Connah's Quay and Buckley Railways, the company shared two rooms in Westminster looked after by George Lewis as secretary of all five. The Aberystwyth & Welsh Coast had offices on the floor below; those of Savin and Benjamin Piercy were nearby. The companies generally held board meetings on the same day while their directors were up from the country. There was plenty of work as by this time the O & N was expanding in several directions at once, both on its own initiative and with the aid of other companies.

FIRST BRANCH LINES

The completion of the Shrewsbury & Welshpool on 27 January 1862 gave the O & N its shortest route to the Midlands and London, but it at once started siphoning off some of the through traffic from the Oswestry line. The S & W had been incorporated in 1856 by the group which broke away from the O & N on its formation, and opened from Shrewsbury to Minsterley on 1 June 1861. The S & W was worked by the LNWR while the GWR also exercised running powers until 1865 when both jointly absorbed the 21-mile line. But this was not the first line to join the O & N, for a few weeks ahead of the completion of the main line there were three branch developments : the opening of the Porthywaen branch on 1 May 1861, and the authorisation of the Llanfyllin and Kerry lines on 17 May. Of these, the Porthywaen was the shortest, running 1¾ miles from just north of Llynclys station to quarries at Porthywaen and White-haven. It was built with a maximum gradient of 1 in 63 along the north side of the Crickheath Tramway and crossed it on the level near the terminus. It was purely a freight line as was a branch which stemmed from it. This linked T. & J. Savin's New British Coal Pit at Coed-y-go, to the north-east. It was a steeply-graded line of just over two miles and it was built privately by the Savin Brothers, who opened it on 31 March 1863. Some twenty coal wagons were worked daily each way until the pit closed in 1869. Although the track was lifted by the eighties, the course of it can still be traced.

The Savins also worked limestone quarries near Porthywaen and, in November 1867, the Cambrian agreed to carry materials free for Savin for him to build an extra wharf at Porthywaen on condition that he built it himself. About a year later the Cambrian threatened to close his freight account and seize his traffic in transit unless he paid outstanding bills. The threat, although made several times, was never carried out.

Savin also figured in the history of the next branch to open—the Kerry, which ran just under four miles through the Mule Gorge in the hills from Abermule. It was built largely on the initiative of a prosperous farmer, John Wilkes, who founded the famous breed of Kerry mountain sheep. He agitated strongly for a line to serve the hills as the O & N was under construction and, on 26 September 1861,

Savin agreed to build the branch on the same terms as the main line. Money was always short and successive calls were made on shares during the whole time up to the opening on 2 March 1863. Yet if money was short during construction, traffic was even scarcer once the line opened, and after only three years the situation got so critical that it went before the board on Christmas Eve 1866. The

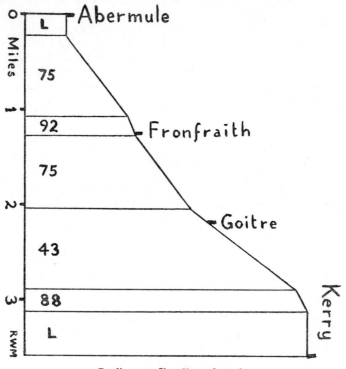

Gradient profile: Kerry branch

decision reached by the directors on that festive eve was nebulous enough: to seek the solicitor's advice about the company's obligations concerning the branch. Whatever he advised, nothing was done and the branch struggled on until an improvement in trade generally brought an improvement in traffic too.

From Abermule, which had a run-round loop and sidings, the line climbed steeply through the narrow gorge and crossed the river five times before reaching a terminus still a mile short of Kerry village.

There was a siding at Middle Mill, near Abermule, and halts, without buildings, at Fronfraith (1¼ miles) and Goitre (2¼ miles). The line included 1,467 yd of 1 in 43 which subsequently became the steepest standard-gauge gradient on which the Cambrian worked passenger trains. Kerry also had a run-round loop, sidings, a small engine shed and a station with a long single platform and cottage-type buildings. There was no intermediate loop on the single line.

Agitation for the Llanfyllin branch was also local, growing in tiny communities living in isolated valleys. Their leader was a local solicitor, John Pugh, whose grandson, O. V. S. Bulleid, spent his childhood at Llanfyllin before growing up to achieve eminence in building locomotives rather than branches.

The agitation was sparked off by a number of schemes being proposed, including in September 1860 one for a line through the area and on to the coast. The West Midland, Shrewsbury & Coast of Wales Railway aimed at building a 90-mile spearhead from the West Midland Railway at Shrewsbury to Portmadoc, *via* Llanymynech. It was projected to pass near Llanfyllin to reach the lead mining village of Llangynog at the head of the neighbouring Tanat valley. From there it was to burrow for nearly two miles under the Berwyns and on through Dolgelley.

The West Midland sent representatives to a town's meeting which the O & N organised at Llanfyllin Town Hall on 13 October 1860 to discuss a branch from Llanymynech. This was decided upon after it was stated to cost about £60,000—five times less than building a branch from anywhere else. Benjamin Piercy and Savin were also at the meeting. The groundwork was done quickly and, on 27 October, the O & N decided to get powers for a branch and also for a line to Llanymynech Lime Rocks, provided subscriptions were forthcoming to finance the first £1,500 of every mile and land-owners agreed to sell their land at agricultural, rather than develop-ment, value—and to take shares in lieu of cash. John Pugh organised a subscription list, setting the pace with £3,000 himself.

The following July, Piercy started planning the route and also that to Kerry. Two months later Savin agreed to build both lines. The Llanfyllin plans displaced a proposal for a short branch to canal wharves at Llanymynech to connect with local quarry tramways. Two years earlier, the O & N had agreed to put in an exchange siding for one of the tramways, for which it was to meet the bill of £480. The O & N was also asked to build a siding to local lime kilns and quarries, handling traffic at special rates. A lodge was also requested for a tramway crossing keeper.

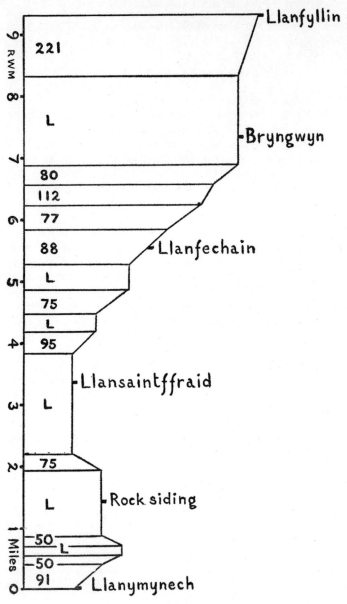

Gradient profile: Llanfyllin branch

The first sod of the Llanfyllin branch was cut at Llwyn, near Llanfyllin, on 20 September 1861 and Savin, then in partnership with his brother-in-law John Ward, quickly built the line. The 9¼ miles were straightforward but the gradients steep, although the rise only involved 240 ft. There was a short stretch of 1 in 50 on each side of the canal crossing. For a line which ran only through fields, its approach to Llanymynech was through a tenuous, back-door route which involved trains reversing twice so as to gain sufficient height to pass over the Shropshire Union Canal. They used a short bay at the north end of the up platform, facing Oswestry, and were propelled from it into a single shunting neck which ran nearly parallel and climbed above the main line. Then they reversed and ran forward, soon crossing over the canal and running alongside Rock Siding serving lime kilns. The branch went on to cross two of the narrow-gauge tramways from Llanymynech Hill to the canal and also the Nantmawr branch.

The first trains ran on 10 April 1863 and there were occasional workings up to the official opening excursion on 17 July. This was not the customary shuttle up and down the new line followed by a directors' bun-fight, but a 23-coach special run to Borth—as far as it was possible to go at that time. It gave many of the 600 passengers from the hilly valley their first view of the sea.

Llansaintffraid was the only intermediate station in o & n days. Another was planned at Llanfechain and, when there was no sign of it being built as opening time approached, the directors hastily asked Savin what was wrong. He explained that he had been unable to get the land, but eventually the station was opened in January 1866, followed a month later by one at Brongwyn (later Bryngwyn). It was unstaffed and passengers operated a signal if they wanted a train to stop. There was one intermediate loop at Llansaintffraid.

Once the branch was opened, fresh moves were made to get a railway to serve another important valley near Oswestry—the Tanat. In September 1863, Robert Piercy surveyed a route for extending the Llanfyllin branch to Llangynog and, although no action was taken at the time, the idea was revived at a special meeting of Cambrian shareholders on 26 April 1873. It failed to find outside support and was abandoned for ever and for 40 years the Llanfyllin branch continued to be the railhead for a large part of rural Montgomeryshire.

Although passenger traffic hardly developed, a heavy goods traffic developed when Liverpool Corporation decided to build a big reservoir at the source of the Vyrnwy in the hills behind the market town in the early eighties. In February 1881, Liverpool proposed to construct a narrow-gauge tramway alongside the road from Llany-blodwell to Penybontfawr to carry materials. The gauge was not to exceed 3 ft 6 in. and steam traction was considered. Nothing was done about the plan and, when work on the dam started in June, materials were taken to Llanfyllin and drawn by horses through the hills. The foundation stone was laid on 14 July 1881.

When the lake was eventually completed on 16 March 1910 it became the biggest in Wales. Cement for the dam and huge pipes for the aqueduct to Liverpool were shipped to Aberdovey and taken by rail to Llanfyllin, where a new siding and storage shed was authorised on 22 July 1882. Large stables for 95 horses were set up in the station yard for the horses hauling materials.

The Llanfyllin branch was also involved in earlier plans for a line from Shrewsbury to Nantmawr promoted in 1862. After several false starts, it was eventually built as the Potteries, Shrewsbury & North Wales Railway and crossed the Cambrian on the level just south of Llanymynech station and passed under the Llanfyllin branch at Wern. A station was built alongside the Cambrian's at Llanymynech and there was a limited interchange of traffic following the opening on 13 August 1866. But the PS & NW was a sickly infant which served country areas even more remote than many around Oswestry and it closed on 21 December. It reopened two years later and at first passenger trains worked between Shrewsbury and Llanymynech only, but they were extended over the Nantmawr branch to Llanyblodwell from 18 April 1870.

A LINK IS SPURNED

Another line which was planned to link up with the O & N was that of the Bishop's Castle Railway, a little concern with big ambitions, of which George Whalley was the main instigator. One of the last acts of the O & N before it merged into the Cambrian was to take powers to subscribe £50,000 towards the BC Railway (as it was often called). Yet the Cambrian never considered doing so for a moment. This was because of strained relations which followed the final meeting of O & N shareholders. It centred on four directors who also formed the majority of the BCR board: Whalley, Wilding, Pearson and Lefeaux. The meeting censured all four, refusing to re-elect the last two and asking the other pair to resign. They agreed to this on condition that the O & N withdrew suits it had lodged against them alleging that they had been trying to create votes.

In retaliation, the four petitioned on the BCR's behalf for running powers over the Cambrian on its formation. It was regarded as a hostile attempt to drain away Cambrian traffic at Montgomery and a Parliamentary committee refused the powers without calling on the Cambrian to state its objections.

This was just another example of nobody taking the BCR's intentions seriously. It always negotiated from a position of puny weakness. It was formed to develop a scheme first suggested in 1859, when the O & N was out of funds, for a cross-country link with the Shrewsbury & Hereford Railway. Incorporated on 28 June 1861, the BCR's main line was to run from the O & N near Montgomery station to Stretford Bridge, north of Craven Arms. Two short branches were planned: from Lydham Heath to Bishop's Castle and the second to Montgomery town. They were needed because to take the main line through Bishop's Castle and Montgomery town would have meant stiff gradients. Construction started in 1863 at the Stretford Bridge end. Progress was slow and to try and speed it up the BCR sought the help of any company it could find which was likely to be interested. Early in 1864, it gave the Aberystwyth & Welsh Coast running powers over its line in return for those between Machynlleth and Aberystwyth. Then, after the rebuff over Cambrian running powers later in the same year, it got powers—on 29 June 1865—for a 9¼-mile branch from Chirbury to the Minsterley branch of the Shrewsbury & Welshpool. The first section of the BCR also stretched 9¼ miles—but from the S & H to Bishop's Castle *via* Lydham. It was formally opened on 24 October 1865, although it seems that public trains did not run for some months because of a dispute with the contractor. The remainder of the line from Lydham to Montgomery was never even started.

By the summer of 1866, the BCR felt relations with the Cambrian had healed sufficiently for it to seek talks on traffic arrangements. The Cambrian board, which met on 20 July, responded by agreeing to a meeting. But it was never held and the next contact of importance was not for another three years until, on 31 August 1869, the BCR wrote to say it was completing a working arrangement with the S & H but having regard to the purpose of its Act, which was to develop traffic over the Cambrian and the Mid Wales Railway, it was incumbent on it to give the Cambrian an opportunity of suggesting terms for working the line. The Cambrian replied that as it was not acquainted with the negotiations with the S & H it could not give an opinion, but it would be pleased to consider any specific proposal of the BCR.

Several times the company asked for help to complete the line through to Montgomery, but the Cambrian, with financial troubles of its own and also its desire not to lose mileage on through traffic *via* Montgomery, was not interested. The first approach on these lines had been from Whalley in October 1873. The Cambrian declined another on 25 August 1876 and a long period elapsed before a fresh initiative, this time from a new company, the Bishop's Castle & Montgomery Railway, incorporated on 7 August 1884. The extension which this new company had been formed to build continued to lack support and it was revived for the last time on 5 July 1887.

CHAPTER 3

Life-line to the Coast

Because so many railways were planned and built simultaneously in mid-Wales, we have run ahead of events and now we return to the period when construction had just started on the O & N and take up the story of another of the Cambrian's constituents which built the main line over the mountains from the Severn Valley to that of the Dovey and to Machynlleth at the threshold of the coast.

The Montgomeryshire railway promoters first started thinking of crossing the mountain in 1856, almost as soon as construction had begun on the Llanidloes & Newtown and the O & N's connecting link to Oswestry. The direct route from the Severn to Aberystwyth, by far the largest of the coast resorts, was blocked by the massive flanks of Plynlimon, and the easiest and obvious route lay through Machynlleth, where the plan was enthusiastically received and backed by a local solicitor, David Howell. A 23-mile line from the L & N near Caersws to Machynlleth was prepared by Benjamin Piercy. It involved a climb of from 412 ft to a summit of 693 ft at Talerddig with a maximum gradient of 1 in 71. There was an even steeper descent to near sea level at Machynlleth with the first four miles at 1 in 52/60. The N & M's birth was heralded by ambitious talk of linking the district with London, Birmingham, Manchester and Liverpool.

A provisional board led by Sir Watkin Williams-Wynn first met at Machynlleth on 27 December 1856 and it was also attended by Howell and Piercy. Following an unopposed passage through Parliament, the Newtown & Machynlleth Railway was incorporated on 27 July 1857 with a capital of £150,000 and loan power for £50,000. Five years were allowed for completion and at first things went well. The chairman congratulated shareholders on 22 August on 'so much having been achieved in so short a period', and pointed out that it was scarcely nine months since the project was announced, and yet, despite many discouraging circumstances (the details were not given), the Act had been obtained without opposition. The improved prospects of the O & N, the progress of work on the Llanidloes line and confidence brought by its own Act were all calculated to be highly beneficial in getting capital subscribed. Six companies—the L & N, O & N, Shrewsbury & Welshpool, GWR, LNWR and SU Canal—had called shareho!ders' meetings and authorised arrangements with the new railway.

The N & M established its headquarters at Machynlleth and Earl Vane, who was not named in the Act because he was a Peer, was elected chairman with Sir Watkin his deputy. David Howell became secretary and Benjamin and Robert Piercy engineers. The line was authorised without a branch and so when the Corris Tramway announced plans to get an Act for extensions in 1858, it was welcomed by the company, which considered an enlarged tramway would be a valuable feeder line. Because it was always conscious that its single thread through the mountains would yield little local traffic, the N & M often took the initiative in promoting ties with other companies. It was a policy which was to end in deep embarrassment and resentment, from which it was only rescued by amalgamation to form the Cambrian.

The tender of Davies and Savin was accepted for construction and the first sod was cut by Countess Vane on the site of Machynlleth station late in November 1858. Davies and Savin started work the following February, but little progress had been made by the time they split in October 1860.

Davies, who was also the main shareholder, continued building the N & M on his own while Savin worked on the line to Aberystwyth, springboard of his ambitious plans to develop the whole of Cardigan Bay northwards. The contractors settled who should work for whom when Davies addressed a meeting of navvies at Machynlleth and told those who wanted to work on the Newtown line to stand on the left; those who preferred the Aberystwyth route, on the right.

The split also meant that Davies was left to fulfil plans to work the N & M separately from the Oswestry and Llanidloes lines and, in 1860, he ordered two 'powerful' locomotives from Sharp, Stewart & Company of Manchester. This plan was changed when the N & M started to play power politics by promoting a Bill in 1861 to amalgamate with the Oswestry and Llanidloes companies. This was withdrawn by mutual consent in 1861, the understanding being that the position would be reviewed before Parliament began its next session.

In the meantime, the situation changed when the other companies made closer ties with the LNWR. The N & M was offended by being left out of talks over working arrangements which it claimed affected it as well. The new ties led the N & M to fear isolation and, to protect itself and its capital outlay, it arranged for the GWR to work the line for 40 per cent of the gross earnings. In addition, the N & M was to be paid for through traffic and shareholders were guaranteed an annual dividend of 5 per cent.

A special meeting of N & M shareholders approved the arrangement on 31 August 1861, but the GWR turned cool and failed to get ratification from its shareholders. The following February the N & M reported that it had been thought best for the GWR to work the line only when it was opened throughout to avoid interference with the contractor's trains. Dividend arrangements, too, were not to start until completion.

To prevent the GWR slipping out of the agreement, the N & M decided in 1862 to promote a Bill to establish the arrangement in perpetuity. With several other Welsh railway Bills, it was not prepared in time and was held over until the following year. The GWR agreed to carry on the arrangement in the interim but, when the line was due to be opened on 3 January 1863, it was announced 'with deep regret' that the GWR had refused to work it because the permanent stations were not complete. The N & M claimed this was due to lack of funds because its Bill had not been ready for the last session of Parliament as the GWR refused to strike out clauses which were described as being 'inserted in its own interests'.

It was also contended that the GWR had ignored an agreement to call shareholders' meetings as quickly as possible to sanction arrangements, while the N & M had done so within 23 days. The N & M lamented that the GWR 'while professing its intention of maintaining the agreement in its integrity, had not taken steps to make it binding'.

The N & M now dropped the GWR plan for fear of antagonising its pro-LNWR neighbours and turned instead to one of them: the O & N, with which it still hoped to amalgamate. Working terms were agreed which were similar to those of the GWR. But they were not quite as attractive, the dividend guarantee being dropped to 4½ per cent. The agreement, arranged under the O & N's 1860 Act, meant that the O & N leased the N & M for 100 years. It was signed on 31 August, and backdated to 1 March 1863, but the line had been worked from its opening on 3 January by Savin & Company under the 1861 O & N Working Agreement.

There was a technical change in lease on 3 December with the formation of the Oswestry & Newtown Joint Committee, which was set up to consolidate the interests of various railways. Savin's lease was ended and the Committee bought the locomotives and rolling-stock from the different companies (including the two locomotives which Davies had bought for the N & M), and then hired them to Savin. This arrangement was regularised by an Act obtained by the O & N as the dominant party in the original lease in 1864 and, on 2 September, Savin received the balance outstanding for the rolling-stock. It was made in 5 per cent preference shares worth £27,977 16s 6d. In addition, certain locomotives were retained by Savin for his own use in constructing new lines and the eventual ownership of this stock later proved difficult to establish.

One of the N & M's last acts before amalgamation with the O & N was to approve a Bill on 3 June 1864 for arrangements with nine companies including the GWR, the Hereford, Hay & Brecon and the Brecon & Merthyr. On amalgamation, Davies and Earl Vane got an agreement which guaranteed the O & N shareholders a $4\frac{1}{2}$ per cent return on ordinary capital and 5 per cent on preference and debentures.

BOG, ROCK AND GOLD

Despite the congratulations given to shareholders in the summer of 1857, there was a long pause in starting construction and, when landowners became difficult, little was done to overcome their opposition. In September 1858 the directors said that while they would have liked to have reported more progress towards starting work, there was no hurry while neighbouring lines remained unfinished. They still had nearly two years to acquire land and four to complete the line.

A single line with several passing loops was decided upon and Davies and Savin's contract was worth £130,000. The first section they started was between the L & N and Talerddig—a stretch of nine miles. It was hoped to complete this in the eleven months from February 1859 when traffic was expected to yield a profit of $3\frac{1}{2}$ per cent, increased to 5 per cent on the opening of the O & N. Once work started, landowners became more co-operative and some accepted rent or shares.

Later in 1859, the Talerddig-Llanbrynmair section was begun, but wet weather and the difficult terrain kept it well behind schedule. The split between Davies and Savin caused further delay on this stretch. Several months later the three miles from the L & N junction

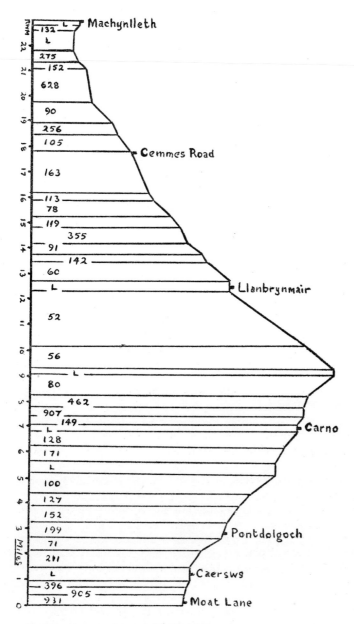

Gradient profile: Newtown & Machynlleth Railway. The summit is Talerddig

to Pontdolgoch were nearly ready, but delays in getting land for Pontdolgoch Cutting until winter had set in caused more trouble. Following heavy rain there were severe slips in this and Talerddig Cutting, on which work had started in 1859.

The section between Carno and Pontdolgoch was finished in a hurry as a tollgate was built on a parallel road which was being used to carry materials for the line. The original plan was for a tunnel at Talerddig, but this was changed when the contractors found they needed a lot of stone to bridge deep ravines. At the time of building, Talerddig was the deepest rock cutting in the world with a depth of 120 ft. A little gold was found by the navvies who were at work on its jagged rock faces until September 1861. The cutting, tapering to a narrow V at track level, is among the most memorable in Britain : from the footplate it seems as if the razor-sharp rocks will shave off the cab sides.

Talerddig was not the only notable engineering feature of the N & M. Immediately west of it, the line was carried lengthwise over the Wynnstay stream and the course of the River Carno through Talerddig bog was diverted and deepened to prevent the line being flooded. Another feature was a substantial timber bridge over the Severn at Caersws. The steepest gradients through the Carno and Dovey valleys to Machynlleth needed heavier track and it was originally laid with double-headed rail on cast-iron chairs while the rest of the line was flat-bottomed rail.

By the summer of 1861 nine miles from Caersws Junction to Talerddig were nearly complete and the next eleven miles were well advanced, although there were gaps until the completion of three heavy bridges over the River Twymyn near Commins Coch. By mid-winter contractors' trains were running over sixteen miles of the route.

Plans to open the line in stages were abandoned early on because of the GWR's attentions. Early in 1860 it had been prematurely announced that the first three miles to Pontdolgoch were open and the likelihood seems to have been that there was an unadvertised and unofficial service over this section. A contractor's train caused great excitement when it reached Machynlleth on 1 May 1862—the day on which Davies had promised it would to mark the opening of the great International Exhibition of that year. But a lot remained to be done and the section from the L & N to Llanbrynmair was not opened, as had been hoped, in time to get summer holiday traffic to the coast quicker than by road. It was January 1863 before the line was finally ready for opening throughout.

STATION STYLES—1

(9) *Borth. Main station buildings dwarfed by Savin's original row of houses practically unaltered after 100 years*

(10) *Llynclys, up side, an original Oswestry & Newtown station, in 1904*

STATION STYLES—2

(11) *Llanymynech, looking south. Derelict 'Potts' station on left. Cambrian cattle trucks in Llanfyllin branch platform*

(12) *End of the main line: Aberystwyth about 1905 with Manchester & Milford train on left*

The ceremonial train on 3 January ran under a triumphal arch at Caersws proclaiming 'Mr Davies for ever', but by then he had left mid-Wales and was building the Pembroke & Tenby. From constructing the N & M, Davies made enough money to diversify and in South Wales he went into coal mining. Considering the difficult country, the N & M had cost a modest £9,000 a mile. There were five intermediate stations: Caersws, Pontdolgoch, Carno, Llanbrynmair and Cemmes Road. The last three had crossing loops.

Within a few years two independent branches off the N & M were promoted and they brought useful extra mineral traffic. The first was the Mawddwy Railway, incorporated on 5 July 1865 and opened from Cemmes Road to Dinas Mawddwy—a distance of 6¾ miles—on 1 October 1867. Connections were soon made with several slate quarries in the Upper Dovey Valley through a network of narrow-gauge tramways. The second branch was the Van Railway, promoted privately by Earl Vane and David Davies in 1870 and opened to the Van lead mines on 14 August 1871, a quarter of a mile less in length than the Mawddwy. Both lines later joined the Cambrian, but now we must pass to the last of the original constituents—the Oswestry, Ellesmere & Whitchurch Railway—which was to provide another outlet to the north.

THE OSWESTRY, ELLESMERE & WHITCHURCH RAILWAY

The last of the four original constituent companies which formed the Cambrian main line, the Oswestry, Ellesmere & Whitchurch, was born after one of the fiercest contests to face the embryo Cambrian. The local company later admitted that it had 'to fight for every inch of the ground'. Yet the first meetings and moves were quiet and straightforward enough. Whalley presided at a public meeting at the Bridgewater Hotel, Ellesmere, on 1 October 1860. The audience was told that not only would the projected line serve the local area, but it would also provide a valuable link between the O & N and Crewe, Manchester and the north. The old skeleton of a line to Milford Haven was brought out of the cupboard and paraded as an extra factor. The completion two years earlier of the LNWR line from Crewe to Whitchurch (it was opened as a single track on 2 September 1858 and was to be doubled in 1862) had encouraged the Welsh promoters in their attempts to find fresh outlets. They also talked of a branch from the OE & W at Ellesmere through Ruabon to the expanding coal and iron area at Ffrith, near Brymbo, which lay to the north-west of Wrexham, and also a

D

branch from Whittington to the GWR at Gobowen.

Local committees were formed at Oswestry, Ellesmere and Whitchurch to raise subscriptions and six days later a provisional committee met for the first time. The Piercy brothers were appointed engineers and George Lewis secretary—but only after they had agreed not to make the committee liable for the cost of any of their preliminary services.

As the days passed it became clear that sufficient money would not be easy to raise, and on 26 October it was decided that the Wrexham (Ffrith) branch would be deposited separately and form no part of the OE & W. In December the promoters heard that the GWR was planning to put Oswestry on its main line to Shrewsbury by converting its branch into a loop and so they dropped plans for the branch from Whittington to Gobowen, although they told the GWR they would build it if they wished.

The OE & W promoters now became anxious to get the scheme moving before the GWR decided to interfere and an urgent call was made for shares to be raised at Oswestry. In the winter of 1860 the first opposition came when the GWR secretary Charles Saunders attacked the company's plans. He said it was both uncalled for and injurious to GWR interests.

On 9 January 1861 T. & J. Savin and Ward were appointed contractors and agreed to meet Parliamentary expenses and deposit and construction costs in excess of £1,500 a mile, provided the promoters got land for at least fifteen of the eighteen miles and the initial money for each mile. Arbitration, if it arose, was to be on the basis of that of the O & N and L & N. Farmers were asked, as usual, to accept agricultural land values, taking part in rent or shares.

The route included several sharp banks at 1 in 80, including two, each over a mile long, on each side of the summit at Frankton.

Later in January 1861 a group of the promoters broke away for a short while and campaigned for a five-mile branch from Bettisfield to Wem on the Whitchurch-Shrewsbury line. They contended that not only would this line have first class stations at each end, but it would be cheap to build, costing no more than £5,000. They envisaged a circle of lines centred on Ellesmere and Hanmer, a village four miles away. This would put Ellesmere ten miles from Whitchurch and Wem; twenty from Shrewsbury; eight from Oswestry and twelve from Wrexham, if that line were built. The promoters turned down the Wem branch when the GWR prepared a counter line from Oswestry to Rednal (putting Oswestry on a main-line

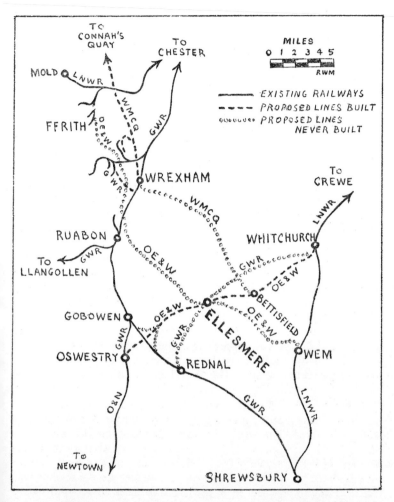

Proposed railways to Ellesmere, 1861. These were not the first: the Shropshire Union Newtown—Crewe route, engineered by Robert Stephenson in 1846 (page 19), included a branch to Ellesmere from the main line, which was to run about a quarter of a mile south of the town.

loop) with a branch from Rednal to Ellesmere. To satisfy local opinion, it was prepared to go on to Whitchurch. Loosely, the GWR said this would give it access to North Wales, although quite how was never detailed. Locally, it was hoped the line would cater for iron, goods and cattle traffic. The OE & W contended that its scheme would help local traffic whatever the competition and serve a more populous area than a line to Shrewsbury.

Local interests lined up behind the different schemes. The OE & W lobbied iron and coal owners around Ruabon, Chirk and Vron. Whitchurch petitioned against the GWR plans, but at Oswestry opinions were divided, while people at Ellesmere were no doubt too confused by the dizzy prospect of an array of lines converging from several directions to take sides.

In Parliament, the OE & W Bill was supported by the LNWR—and strenuously opposed by the GWR as the line would mean that north-bound traffic from the Montgomeryshire railways would be routed via the LNWR from Whitchurch instead of over the GWR from Oswestry. Even worse was the threat of a line to Ffrith, which would cut right across the GWR's exclusive preserve of the industrial area around Wrexham. With the Wem branch it would provide a through route from Mold and Chester to the LNWR at Shrewsbury and on to the midlands and south independent of the GWR. The GWR claimed its plan would provide a more effective link between Elles-mere and Shrewsbury and also between Ellesmere and Ruabon. The OE & W said that it was not aiming at Shrewsbury or Ruabon, but if a rail link between them was needed, then it could suggest a better one than that of the GWR. The Wrexham branch would be started as soon as the main line was completed.

The outcome of the battle was Parliament's rejection of the GWR Bill and its approval of that of the OE & W. But the Act of 1 August 1861 stipulated that work was only to start on the Ellesmere-Whitchurch section. That from Ellesmere to Oswestry was suspended until 1 September 1862, under a clause inserted by the Lords. It was aimed at a reconciliation with the GWR to see if a scheme was forthcoming to link four local towns: Ellesmere, Oswestry, Ruabon and Shrewsbury.

The Act allowed five years for completion and provided for a capital of £150,000 and £50,000 in loans. Of that, £18,000 had already been spent on the Parliamentary battle.

When the news of the OE & W Act reached Ellesmere, nobody could be found to ring the church bells, but at Oswestry they pealed for two days. While the OE & W supporters were jubilant, those of the GWR suffered an indignity—at the hands of the GWR! For they were left behind at Paddington when the coach in which they were travelling home was not coupled up to a Shrewsbury express.

The OE & W, which set up offices at Oswestry, followed up the Lords' hopes of reconciliation by writing to the GWR on 31 October offering co-operation in building junctions at Whittington, where their lines crossed, provided that there was no interference with the concept of a through route to link the O & N at Oswestry with Staffordshire and Lancashire. The GWR replied naively that it could not understand what the OE & W was talking about. The OE & W interpreted this as a GWR desire to re-open the whole contest and substitute its own line from Oswestry to Ellesmere via Rednal.

Whalley saw danger from another source. He felt it might come from Lord Brownlow, a local landowner, who doubted the company's ability to pay. But the Act also empowered the LNWR to subscribe £30,000. In return, it was to have running powers and the right (with the GWR) to have its own staff at stations if it wanted. The OE & W was granted the same rights at Whitchurch and Crewe and intermediate LNWR stations, but not running powers. There was no concession regarding GWR running powers over the OE & W.

Before construction started, the engineers were asked to re-survey the Ellesmere-Oswestry section to meet the wishes of some landowners, and also to make preliminary surveys to Ruabon and Shrewsbury. On 17 August 1861, the bailiffs at Ellesmere went to a board meeting which discussed ways of cutting the first sod in the 'most public manner'. This was done by Sir John Hanmer, M.P., at Ellesmere on 29 August. Not to be outdone, Oswestry had its own ceremony a year later when work started on the section west of Ellesmere. (See p. 10.)

Work got under way on 4 September and three days later Savin & Company asked for £10,000 to meet Parliamentary expenses, the cost of buying land and carrying out preliminary works. As the OE & W had no funds, the O & N was asked to take up £10,000 in shares and pay Savin. The request was again made a month later when Savin wanted more money. George Owen was appointed resident engineer under the Piercys on 25 September.

The start of construction brought fresh pressure from industrialists in the Wrexham and Mold areas for a branch through Wrexham to the Mold line and, on 24 October 1861, the OE & W decided to publish Parliamentary notices for the line from Ellesmere to Ruabon, with a branch to Wrexham. It also revived the Bettisfield-Wem plan for, besides serving local interests, this would also form a second link between Ellesmere and Shrewsbury which would be almost as short as the proposed GWR line. The Wem branch got through Parliament on 7 August 1862 and allowed three years for completion. The Ffrith branch was thrown out and never revived. The Wem scheme fared little better for construction was never started and the powers were allowed to lapse when they ran out on 5 July 1865.

BOG AND BRUSHWOOD

Within six months of the start of work on the Ellesmere-Whitchurch line, most of the track had been laid and locomotives tested on its most difficult stretch—the crossing of Whixall Moss—a bog almost three miles broad, which is often compared to that of Chat Moss on the Liverpool & Manchester Railway. The line was taken over Whixall Moss to avoid the property of Sir John Hanmer. When it was threatened by GWR plans, he became a staunch supporter of the OE & W.

It was impossible to drain the Moss to get a firm track foundation. While the average depth was estimated to be only about 12 ft, a surveyor lost a 35 ft rod trying to find the bottom in one place. Finally the line was built on a raft of brushwood, supported on timbers, 12 ft by 3 ft, and topped with sand ballast.

By the end of August 1862 the Ellesmere-Whitchurch section was complete, apart from two short lengths of track at each end. The Moss had been fully tested by the shuttling of heavy ballast trains across it. In contrast to the early enthusiasm to build a line there was little desire to open it and the section lay unused until the following Spring when goods started running on 20 April 1863. It was followed by a passenger service on 4 May. By then, the OE & W's turntable and station accommodation at Whitchurch had been completed, as well as intermediate stations at Welshampton, Bettisfield and Fenn's Bank, all without crossing facilities.

Meanwhile, during the previous autumn, work had started on the seven-and-a-half-mile section west from Ellesmere to Oswestry. It began on 4 September 1862—only three days after the date authorised in the original Act. There were no major obstacles and Savin pressed on quickly and when the Borth-Aberystwyth section opened on 23 June 1864, it left this section as the only unfinished one over the 96 miles from Whitchurch to the coast. That gap was closed on 27 July 1864—two days after the OE & W had become part of the Cambrian. At first Whittington was the only intermediate station between Ellesmere and Oswestry (above and a little distance from

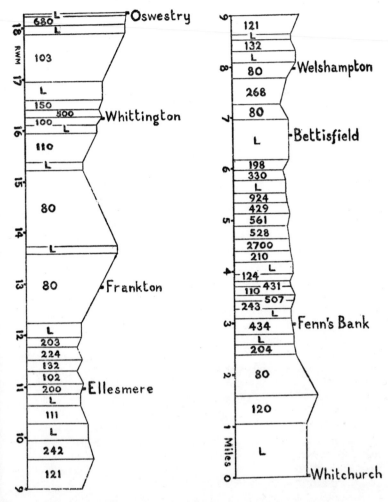

Gradient profile: Oswestry, Ellesmere & Whitchurch Railway

the GWR station). Frankton, serving the twin Border villages of English Frankton and Welsh Frankton, was added in 1866. Ellesmere was the only intermediate station with a passing loop. Permanent stations were not built at Fenn's Bank and Frankton until the early eighties.

In December 1868 it had been decided to move the platform at Whittington from the south side to the north of the line—provided it did not cost more than £6.

The railway pattern in the area was completed by the OE & W. Three more lines were projected before promoters finally lost interest in the Border country. One was for a direct line from Wrexham to Whitchurch, for which the Wrexham, Mold & Connah's Quay got powers on 25 July 1864. It was routed through Bangor on Dee to Bettisfield and included running powers over the OE & W and LNWR between the branch junction and Whitchurch station. A further Act of 15 August 1867 extended completion time until 1870, but no work started and the branch was abandoned by Board of Trade warrant on 7 November 1873.

A scheme associated with the WMCQ extension plan was that of the Drayton Railway Company incorporated on 29 July 1864 to construct a line from Prees, via Market Drayton to the Shropshire Union Railway Stafford-Wellington line near Stafford. It planned working arrangements with six companies including the OE & W but never got beyond the planning stage.

The third scheme was for yet another line to Ellesmere, but it was more limited in its object than earlier plans. It was born in 1866 with the formation of the Ellesmere & Glyn Valley Railway, which sought a line, almost certainly standard-gauge, to provide an outlet for busy quarries in the Glyn Valley (birthplace of the Van Railway's poet-manager John Ceiriog Hughes). The company, which wanted working arrangements with the Cambrian and the GWR, planned its route down the south bank of the Glyn Valley and over the GWR and Shropshire Union Canal and on across country to Ellesmere, a total distance of thirteen miles. The scheme was led by Benjamin Piercy with Robert as engineer, but no progress had been made by the time the Regulation of the Railways Act, which introduced the light railway, was passed in 1868. Its effect was immediate and the E & GV got an Act in 1869 to abandon its route between the SU Canal and Ellesmere. On 10 August 1870, the E & GV was dissolved and in its place the Glyn Valley Tramway was incorporated. It was to be built to a gauge of 2 ft 4½ in. Terminating besides the canal at Trehowell, it remained remote and was managed by the canal company for a time. Later it built a new route to Chirk, where it had a station alongside that of the GWR.

CHAPTER 4

Conquering the Coast

THE ABERYSTWYTH & WELSH COAST RAILWAY

The hindsight which history provides makes it clear that any hopes of mid-Wales railways developing into great traffic arteries were dead long before the lines were even conceived. The crucial decision was making Holyhead the Irish packet port. Its geographical position was strategically so strong that nobody seriously considered building an alternative line to the Welsh coast for some years. The first scheme to follow the Chester & Holyhead Railway's development was the Manchester & Milford of 1845.

The promoters of early railways clutched at any straw that might bring them traffic and it was this tactic which put a group working to promote the Corris Railway among the first to consider exploiting railways along the Cambrian coast. The stimulation came from the LNWR-inspired scheme of 1852 for a Shrewsbury-Aberystwyth link and they responded by outlining a route for a standard-gauge railway from the Corris slate quarries down the valley to join it at Machynlleth. From there the Corris plan was to run along the coast to Aberdovey and Towyn.

When the Montgomeryshire Railway's scheme over Talerddig was abandoned, the Corris returned to its shell and its plans were truncated to a local line of eleven miles and of narrow (2 ft 3 in.) gauge. It was to run from Aberllefeni through Machynlleth to a wharf on the south bank of the Dovey estuary at Derwenlas. The Act for the Corris, Machynlleth & River Dovey Tramroad was passed on 12 July 1859 and the line, only horse-drawn, was opened to slate traffic the following year.

But an 'English' line was getting near and plans for it were revived in the year the Corris opened, by a scheme launched by the West Midland, Shrewsbury & Coast of Wales Railway for a link from Shrewsbury to Portmadoc via Llangynog and Bala. The main attraction was Porth Dinlleyn, and when the West Midland scheme was still under discussion there came one for the Portmadoc & Porth

Dinlleyn Railway. Both were rejected by Parliament on Standing Orders in 1861.

Now that revived ambitions for Irish traffic were dying, promoters turned their attention to exploiting Cardigan Bay and its wide, sandy, mountain-framed beaches. The key resort then was, undoubtedly, Aberystwyth, which already had a population of 5,000 and was a centre of regional, as well as local, importance. It had a network of coach services, which ran daily the 72 miles to Shrewsbury and 60 miles to Kington, with Rhayader as the 'half-way house'. Every other day coaches ran 80 miles to Hereford through Builth, and northwards to Machynlleth, Dolgelley, Carnarvon and Oswestry (66 miles). South, there was a service to Carmarthen (51 miles: terminus, 'The Ivy Bush'). There were daily omnibuses to Devil's Bridge.

No wonder that the Newtown & Machynlleth Railway had from its earliest days always regarded Machynlleth as a temporary terminus and its heart and sights were always set on the coast. But the scheme that grew out of its ideas was to be the one which caused so much trouble and resulted in the rift between Davies and Savin. When the Aberystwyth & Welsh Coast Railway was incorporated on 22 July 1861, it was in the face of bitter opposition from the N & M and the West Midland. The N & M succeeded during the Bill's passage through Parliament in getting a clause inserted that if the A &WC failed, and was unable to open the Machynlleth-Aberystwyth section by the completion date of 1 August 1864, then the N & M was to take over the uncompleted works and finish them.

Whalley was appointed chairman of the A & WC; Benjamin Piercy engineer and W. Roberts secretary. The Savin brothers were the contractors. The line was authorised in five parts:

1 Aberystwyth to Penmochno Embankment at Llangynfelyn, near Ynyslas
2 Llangynfelyn to Towyn
3 Towyn to Barmouth
4 Barmouth to Portmadoc
5 Llangynfelyn to the N & M at Machynlleth

The capital of £400,000 was backed by loans of £133,000 and, despite the N & M's hostility, the new company had allies further east with the O & N having subscription powers of £75,000; the L & N of £25,000, and the Act provided for agreements with the Mid Wales Railway and the Shrewsbury & Welchpool, as it was spelt.

Three years were laid down for the compulsory purchase of land, and four for completion of all but railway No 4 (Barmouth-Portmadoc), for which an extra year was allowed. Railway No 1 was not to be made 'more expeditiously' than Nos 2 and 3, north of the Dovey.

Besides the clause about completion, the N & M also got detailed safeguards. The junction at Machynlleth was to be made to its satisfaction and clause 38 stated:

> The *Machynlleth* Company may from Time to Time erect such Signals and Conveniences incident to the Junction, and appoint and remove such Watchmen, Switchmen, or other Persons, as may be necessary for the Prevention of Danger to or Interference with the Traffic at and near the said Junction; and the working and Management of such Signals and Conveniences, whether on the Land of the *Machynlleth* Company or on Land of the [A & WC] Company, shall be under the exclusive Management and Regulation of the *Machynlleth* Company. . .

The A & WC was to pay for the erection and maintenance of the signals and the wages of the watchmen and switchmen.

More far reaching were the conditions laid down by the Admiralty, for as clause 19 stated:

> Where the Railways skirt the Shore of any Sea, River or Estuary, the Railways and other Works shall not deviate waterward from the continuous Centre Line of Way marked on the Plans deposited at the Admiralty without the previous Consent of the Lord High Admiral of the United Kingdom of *Great Britain and Ireland*.

The Lord High Admiral had power to remove any unauthorised deviations and charge the A & WC for the work. He had to approve plans for viaducts or crossings of the rivers Dovey, Mawddach, Artro, Tractbach, Glaslyn and Droyfor and of Pwllheli harbour.

The company was to provide navigation lights on all bridges and viaducts 'for ever', facing a penalty of £10 for every night on which they were not lit. A £10 penalty was also laid down if the A & WC detained any 'Vessel, Barge or Boat' navigating the Dovey estuary for longer than the time needed to allow the passage of a train across the Dovey bridge. Trains were not to shunt across or stand on the eight level crossings and a 'First-class' station for passengers, cattle and goods, 'with a siding and shed' was to be built at Bow Street. An up and down goods was to call daily except Sunday, as well as passenger trains. It was also decreed that the Aberystwyth & Welsh Coast Railway must not build an 'Inn or Eating House' within a mile of the station.

Plans were worked out in secret and when a director, David Williams, asked for minutes of board meetings to be sent to absent colleagues, the request was refused because it was felt there would be great risks if the plans got undue or premature publicity.

Soon after its formation, the A & WC had to start countering threats from other companies, of which the most powerful was the GWR. Although it was still a long way away, it was advancing slowly along the Dee valley from Ruabon. As Dolgelley lay in its path, the A & WC decided to seek powers for a branch to the town. The GWR had reached Llangollen on 1 December 1861, although the company camouflaged its coastal aims at resorts like Barmouth and Aberystwyth by promoting a series of nominally independent lines through the Dee valley, which were to lead to a line over the hills.

It was to run from Bont Newydd (east of Dolgelley) to Machynlleth and include the conversion of the Corris Railway to standard gauge. It was to have a tunnel over a mile long and other heavy engineering works and as a result the idea was soon forgotten. But the Dee Valley lines went ahead from Llangollen to Bala Lake and through the Afon Wnion valley. There were no difficulties in getting land as the principal landowner in the area was a GWR director, Sir Watkin Williams-Wynn. Because of subsequent developments, it is worth tracing briefly the growth of the little lines. The short branch from Ruabon to Llangollen had been built by the Vale of Llangollen Railway and opened to goods on 1 December 1861 (passengers following on 2 June 1862).

As it was being extended to Corwen, the town was reached from the north by the Denbigh, Ruthin & Corwen Railway, on which construction had started in September 1860. It was built and worked by Savin and completed to Corwen in September 1864. The Llangollen & Corwen Railway, just over ten miles long, was opened on 8 May 1865.

Now we go back three years to 29 July 1862, the date on which the A & WC got its Dolgelley branch Act and also powers to extend from Portmadoc to Porth Dinlleyn. On the same day the Carnarvonshire Railway was incorporated to extend the LNWR's Carnarvon branch for twenty-seven and three-quarter miles to Portmadoc. A year later the A & WC tried to take over the line and, although this failed, the A & WC's position was strengthened when it was found that both Acts covered the same route between Afon Wen and Portmadoc. The duplication was ignored at first, but the position was finally resolved by an agreement of 13 December 1865 under which the Cambrian built the section.

The A & WC's only other attempt at expansion was through a plan to build a branch to Ffestiniog. It was planned in November 1862, thrown out by Parliament on 27 August 1863 in the face of opposition from the Festiniog Railway and local quarry owners and nothing more was heard of it.

Due to the N & M's clause, the section from Machynlleth to Aberystwyth was tackled first. Savin was ready to start work in January 1862 and it went ahead so fast that by August all but two miles of the easy marsh crossing alongside the Dovey estuary from Machynlleth to Borth were finished. The main difficulty was crossing the Corris Tramway on the level without interfering with its traffic. With the onslaught of autumn storms work near Borth got tougher and slower and extra police were drafted into the area to keep the peace among the navvies. The Chief Constable of Cardigan, Captain Freeman, asked for payment towards the cost of the extra men, but the A & WC replied that it had no funds available for the purpose. Eight small boats landed the last sleepers in the area on 4 May 1863 and the section to Borth was opened on 1 July. The little village amid the sand dunes then became the coast bridgehead of all the railways of mid-Wales. Through trains *via* the N & M brought visitors in their hundreds—and most of them were seeing the sea for the first time. The two intermediate stations, Glandovey and Ynys-las (as originally spelt), both had crossing facilities.

North of the Dovey work began at Towyn in April 1862, the first sod being cut by Mrs John Foulkes, the wife of a director. The five miles between Aberdovey and the River Dysynni to the north were completed by late summer. Winter gales then delayed progress in building the line along the exposed coast, which included several short grades of 1 in 70/82, and it was not until 24 October 1863 that the first trains ran, made up of engines and coaches ferried across the Dovey from Ynyslas. The same ferry was used by passengers who wanted to continue their journey north from Ynyslas. A temporary siding to the landing stage at Ynyslas was used for trans-shipping goods.

Additional traffic came to Towyn with the opening of the 2 ft 3 in gauge Talyllyn Railway late in 1865. The first scheme for such a line had been outlined at the end of 1862 after the Bryn Eglwys quarries were acquired by the Aberdovey Slate Company. Encouraged by the success of the Corris, the slate company drafted a line to Aberdovey, which was the nearest port. It was routed down the valley to Towyn and along the coast, but early in 1865 this plan was cut back to Towyn, where the Talyllyn was to share a terminus with the proposed Corris, Machynlleth, Aberdovey & Towyn Railway—a short-lived revival of the Corris' 1852 scheme. When that was abandoned because of the A & WC's arrival, the Talyllyn limited its powers to a wharf alongside the main line at Towyn. Its Act of 5 July 1865 also authorised a mixed-gauge spur to the A & WC goods station. This avoided a main-line crossing envisaged in the earlier scheme. The spur powers were allowed to lapse in 1870 when it became clear that little passenger traffic would develop. Liaison between the companies remained active and, in 1912, the Cambrian agreed to a telephone link with Wharf station (now being used by the Talyllyn's passengers), provided it did not cost more than £4 10s to install and £1 10s a year to maintain.

Other storms were gathering, fomented by bitter resentment which Whalley felt towards Savin for his methods of financing the A & WC. It came to a head on 26 November 1863 at a time when Savin had been paid in shares totalling £239,000 for work completed and he was in a powerful position. Whalley and the board tried vainly to limit his power by laying down conditions which were intended to stop him using his shares in voting against the directors, or in any scheme in which he had an interest. One clause withheld any voting rights on shares sold by Savin, with a penalty for default, although subject to arbitration. His proposed contract also included penalties if the Borth-Aberystwyth section was not completed by 1 March 1864 and the viaduct between Ynyslas and Aberdovey by January 1865. They meant that Savin was to pay himself for any work on these projects completed after these dates.

Savin refused the contract and threatened to bankrupt the railway. On 25 February 1864, Whalley appealed for the shareholders' help and also that of the Oswestry and Llanidloes companies. It brought little response and Savin was supported by Henry Gartside, who was also on the O & N board, and J. W. Johns, also an L & N director. Whalley and three other directors were forced to resign and the new board of the A & WC was led by David Williams of Castel Deudraeth. One of the first things he did was to appoint a share-holders' committee to investigate the company's affairs and to ask for the resignation of Benjamin Piercy, who had supported Whalley. He refused to resign and so, with his brother, he was sacked. The new engineer, appointed in March, was Henry Coneybeare from the Brecon & Merthyr.

When things settled down, the O & N offered to work the Machyn-lleth-Aberystwyth section for 45 per cent of the gross receipts; that between Aberdovey and Llwyngwril at actual cost. The inclusion of the Borth-Aberystwyth section was made on the expectation of it being opened within three months.

Eventually on 11 June—seven weeks before the statutory completion date—the eight-and-a-half miles from Borth to Aberystwyth were ready for inspection. It was a section of switchback gradients including five miles at 1 in 76 or steeper, with a maximum of 1 in 60. The route was selected to carry the line over hills behind steep cliffs between Borth and Aberystwyth. Both the intermediate stations at Llanfihangel and Bow Street had loops. The line was opened on 23 June. Derwenlas also had a loop originally.

The opening of the Machynlleth-Aberystwyth line hit the Corris Tramroad by making redundant the section west from Machynlleth to the Dovey wharves at Derwenlas. These were the busy hub of local trade for many years and the Corris promoters thought it worth while to link up with them because they used to handle up to eighty small boats on a single tide.

For a short time the Corris reconsidered plans for a standard-gauge line across the mountains to the GWR but the idea was quickly dropped without a survey being made. The powers which the Corris did get were modest: they were for purely an extension of the narrow-gauge system to Tyr Stint, near Dolgelley. First proposed in 1863, it included two tunnels and gradients of up to 1 in 45. It was never built.

Under the Act—of 25 July 1864—the Corris also got powers to abandon the Machynlleth-Derwenlas section. Yet the Cambrian's working timetables showed the level crossing with the Corris for many years afterwards.

On 26 April 1865 the A & WC decided to take over the Corris, offering £21,000 in preference shares, but, as amalgamation with the Cambrian was pending, nothing more came of the move. The Corris remained independent and there was never any suggestion in the Cambrian's board minutes that the take-over idea should be revived. The Corris always seemed to have good relations with the big companies and when it wanted fresh powers in 1865 it got them through clauses in the A & WC's (General) Act of 5 July. These gave the Corris powers to repeal sections in the original Act forbidding it to carry passengers or run trains faster than 10 m.p.h.

LEFT IN THE COLD

Within five weeks of the opening to Aberystwyth the other end of the main line was completed between Oswestry and Ellesmere and through running from Whitchurch started on 27 July 1864. The Cambrian's creation two days earlier left the A & WC out in the cold. But the reasons were legal, rather than unfriendly. One was because the A & WC could not conform to Commons' Standing Orders in time. The exclusion was also in deed rather than fact for, because of the heavy financial involvement of both the Oswestry and Llanidloes companies in the coast, the Cambrian was asked to work it. It agreed to do so, through Savin & Company, for 45 per cent of the gross receipts. An agreement, dated 12 October 1864, was to run for 14 years unless, it was stated, amalgamation intervened. When the A & WC discussed this agreement, it minuted it as being for 21 years—and back-dated it to 1 July 1863, the date Savin & Company first started to work the line.

Once Aberystwyth was reached progress on building the rest of the coast line lost momentum. One reason was the shortage of money and the Cambrian was asked to exercise its option to contribute £100,000. It agreed on 27 January 1865, but not all the money was paid at once for on 30 March, Savin wrote asking for the balance 'as I am going on very rapidly with the works and the money is very much wanted'. A further £25,000 was then taken in preference shares, increasing the Cambrian's total commitment to a value of £75,000.

North of Llwyngwril progress was slow because of the difficulties of carving the trackbed out of almost sheer cliffs dropping down from Cader Idris at the notorious Friog Rocks. Savin engaged seamen to help in the work. The line was carried along the cliffs at a height of 86 ft above the rock-strewn shore and the approaches were up to 1 in 55. The line opened to Penmaenpool on 3 July 1865 and passengers going north used a temporary station called Barmouth Ferry, on which site Fairbourne station was later built. They walked on across the sand-bar to catch a ferry over the Mawddach estuary to Barmouth harbour. Barmouth Ferry was the only intermediate station on the Penmaenpool section and it did not have a crossing loop.

The next stage to be tackled was the long one between Barmouth and Pwllheli but the going was easier as the coastal strip of flat land widened north of Barmouth. Few earthworks were needed between Barmouth and Portmadoc, apart from a short cutting at Minffordd, but what did have to be built were a number of lengthy viaducts. It is for these that the coast line is renowned as one of the finest in Britain. Barmouth viaduct is superlative, not only as the Cambrian's finest engineering work, but also as the longest in Wales and,

LOCOMOTIVES—GOODS

(13) No. 6 'Marquis' about 1885 with wooden cab sides (no roof), handbrake only and tender panels separately lined out

(14) 'Queen' 0—6—0 No. 34A with new cab and steam brake at Barmouth about 1906

(15) Oswestry & Newtown Railway 0—6—0 'Cambria' as built in 1863

LOCOMOTIVES—TANK

(16) *No. 59 'Seaham' 2—4—0T as running, still unaltered, about 1885*

(17) *No. 13 0—6—0T in later years, modified with metal brake blocks and Aston chimney*

(18) *No. 3 0—4—2ST, with cab added, shunting outside Oswestry Works about 1888*

scenically, as one of the most breathtaking in Britain. To conquer the 800 yd wide mouth of the Mawddach estuary with its treacherous sands, the rails were carried on 113 spans supported by over 500 timber piles, and to maintain a right of way for shipping through a channel on the Barmouth shore there was an iron section of eight spans, including one which drew back on wheels over the others. The viaduct was first tested in July 1866 by the crossing of the 'Albion' 2—4—0 *Mazeppa*, but it was not until 3 June 1867 that a service started—and then only of a horse-drawn carriage. Steam trains did not use it regularly until the opening of the entire coast line four months later. The bridge was not built without a toll in human lives. Two men were lost when a small boat capsized and they were swept away by the tide. There was a sequel to this accident when two workmates appeared at the Spring Assizes at Bala in 1866, accused of their manslaughter.

Completion of the bridge badly hit the trade of local ferrymen and they suffered still further when a footpath—which has proved to be such a magnificent promenade—was built alongside the line under the Cambrian New Works Order of 1868. As compensation for loss of earnings, the ferrymen asked in 1879 for £100—equivalent to four years' rent.

Other major engineering works on the northern section included timber viaducts over the Dysynni and the Dwyryd estuary. The Cambrian also built a toll road alongside the latter which still earns revenue.

Also still in use is an old road toll bridge at Penmaenpool, which the Cambrian bought. One of the worst obstacles had been tamed before the railway arrived. This was the tidal basin of the River Glaslyn at the approach to Portmadoc, reclaimed by the building of the Traeth Mawr embankment—used by the Festiniog Railway. The coast line was driven across marshes about a quarter of a mile behind the embankment and only a small viaduct was needed to cross the Glaslyn as it tumbled from Snowdonia into the sea.

By the time all these viaducts were completed, the A & WC was firmly in the Cambrian camp. It came about with the passing of the Cambrian and Coast Railways (Amalgamation) Act of 5 July 1865, by which the take-over was effected on 5 August 1866. The Bill was opposed by the LNWR, the GWR and its satellite, the Vale of Llangollen Railway, and the Mid Wales Railway, mainly because all were anxious to make sure of running powers over the coast. When the Bill was before a Lords' Select Committee in June 1865, Captain J. W. Johns, deputy chairman of the Cambrian and the A & WC, said

E

the aim was to achieve greater economy by avoiding the duplication of staff. Amalgamation would also mean more efficiency over the whole system and this would help the public.

WITH HASTE, WITHOUT CEREMONY

By amalgamation, work was under way to conquer another obstacle—the Dovey estuary. During the early days of the A & WC's construction, the bleak, exposed and shifting sands defied all efforts to cross them with a viaduct from Ynyslas to Aberdovey. Borers were able to work only when the tide was out and they were unable to find any foundations on which to rest piers—not, perhaps, surprising since when the tide was in, they were in the local pubs!

Gradually the idea was explored of taking the line round the estuary and, once Aberystwyth was reached, the A & WC decided upon this course, only to incur the wrath of the GWR whose coastal ambitions were still contained within the upper reaches of the Dee valley.

There was another stumbling block besides the GWR (and the estuary itself). Interests at Aberdovey carefully, rather than jealously, guarded the shipping trade to which Aberdovey owed its growth, importance and wealth. Great hopes were pinned on the harbour, described to a Commons committee in 1865 as of the greatest national importance and 'equal to Portsmouth'.

The railway's proposed route along the sea front was contested so hotly—partly because of the fear that any bridges might restrict the size of ships able to dock—that it was forced to go round the back of the town. This meant building a tunnel and altogether there were four on the deviation: Frongoch (199¾ yd), Morfor (219 yd), Penhellyg (119 yd) and Craig-y-Don (533 yd). There was scarcely a single length of straight rail. The maximum gradient was 1 in 98, partly in two of the tunnels.

All this extra expense hastened Savin's collapse and was partly responsible for a gap of several years between the railway's arrival at this small port and its opening. Yet this was one of the main centres from which the early visionaries hoped to reap rich traffic! There were also other misgivings about both the original Dovey embankment scheme and the deviation. The embankment was also seen as a hazard to shipping.

Although Parliament allowed the deviation to be built under the A & WC (General) Act of 5 July 1865, it was sufficiently impressed with the GWR's objections to give it a ten-year loophole with powers to build its own bridge across the Dovey. The A & WC's Act stipulated that there was to be no increase in charges to cover the increased mileage (12) which coast trains would have to run. The third-class fare between Aberdovey and Ynyslas was not to exceed sixpence and all other charges, including those for animals, were to be calculated at not more than six miles. On the south bank of the Dovey, a line was authorised to a landing stage at Cerig-y-Penrhyn. The viaduct which the deviation replaced would have rivalled the Barmouth crossing in grandeur and although the viaduct built to carry the deviation across the river near Glandovey Junction was small in comparison, it was still sizeable. While it was built mainly of timber, it had an iron opening span of 35 ft on a drawbridge principle like that at Barmouth.

The deviation Act also gave the A & WC powers for a number of diversions and branches to tidy up the route originally planned. There were powers for short diversions at Llanaber and Llandecwyn, a branch of about one-third of a mile to Aberdovey Wharf, an embankment on the north side of the Dovey, an inner harbour at Portmadoc—the last clause including safeguards for Festiniog Railway interests.

Fresh hopes of an early completion came with amalgamation, especially when it was reported on 29 July 1865 that a contract price of £17,500 a mile, including expenses, had been agreed. But such plans received a setback with Savin's failure on 5 February 1866. Among other things, it left the A & WC faced with the question of who should complete the construction. Brassey was considered, but it was left to Henry Coneybeare and by June 1866 the Board of Trade was told that the whole line, except for the Barmouth viaduct, was ready for first inspection.

But money was tight and the following month plans were upset when the Cambrian was taken to Chancery over claims for land worth £100,000 and as a result the opening was postponed. But this was likely in any case for the Board of Trade Inspector, Captain Tyler, reported in September that the state of the Dovey deviation was not satisfactory. As the four short tunnels had only limited clearance, the Board of Trade insisted on opening carriage windows being fitted with bars. (The only other tunnel was a short one at Barmouth between the station and the bridge.)

To keep down cash payments, landowners were again asked to accept rent rather than demand cash, but for the next fifteen months the track was virtually unused and became almost derelict. The only trains reported were a few local ones which ran at night when

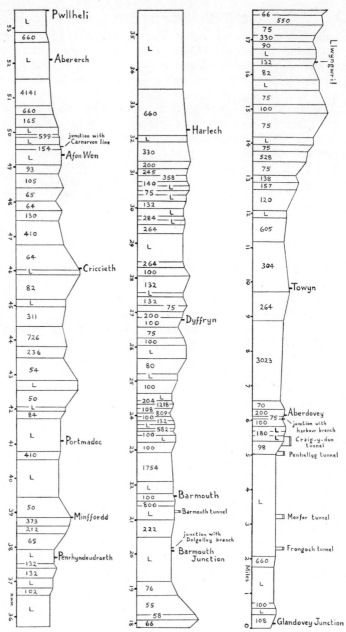

Gradient profile: the coast line to Pwllheli

bailiffs engaged by creditors were asleep. There were other troubles too: in board minutes of 17 November 1866, which were crossed out before the chairman signed them, Coneybeare was sacked and replaced by the Cambrian's engineer, George Owen.

The winter passed without action and the following March the board reviewed the position caused by Savin's inability to complete the line. They wrote to his inspectors pointing out the great sacrifice of interest not only to the company but to his estate as well. At the same meeting the board approved a Carnarvonshire Railway Bill which was to give the Cambrian running powers to Carnarvon (as it was spelt until 1925), in exchange for rights between Portmadoc and Pwllheli. The powers, restricted to through traffic, were conditional on the Cambrian withdrawing its opposition to the Bill, which was passed on 25 July 1867.

It was around this time that events moved to a climax and resulted in the opening of the entire coast line. The first 'break through' was the start of the horse carriage service across Barmouth viaduct followed more solidly by the opening of the Glandovey deviation, which linked up with the long isolated section between Aberdovey and Penmaenpool, on 14 August 1867.

Still, pressing claims by landowners held up the entire opening. In a desperate bid to meet them and get trains running, the board held a special meeting on 24 September and voted to sell all unused materials lying along the line to raise the money for payments. Next came a feeler from the Carnarvonshire Railway, which reached Afon Wen on 2 September, and at once offered to work the Portmadoc-Pwllheli section. The Cambrian said no.

The decision to open the whole line on 10 October was taken by the Cambrian directors only two days before after hearing counsel's advice. The board went on record with several points 'to avoid prejudice and preserve the rights of the interests of the several sections of the Railway'.

1 That land had not been purchased in accordance with the contract, but that rent charges had been created without any provision for a reduction in capital to limit them.

2 The works were generally defective, especially at Friog Cutting, the Aberdovey Tunnel and the 'extensive wooden viaduct'.

3 It had been reported that securities had been given to the contractor or his inspector largely in excess of work done under contract. The Board felt the Act required the coast section to discharge these liabilities.

The haste with which the decision to open was taken meant that trains started running without ceremony. There were no inter-mediate stations on the Glandovey deviation but new stations were brought into use at each end on its opening, both without goods facilities. Glandovey Junction was purely a passenger interchange station set in a remote part of the Dovey marshes, close to tide and wind; far from roads, villages and people. Within sight lay the boundary of three counties: Montgomery, Merioneth and Cardigan. Aberdovey station was built at the junction with the Harbour branch and the original terminus was closed to passengers and the ferry to Ynyslas abandoned. Further north there were crossing stations at Barmouth, Dyffryn, Harlech, Penrhyndeudraeth, Port-madoc, Criccieth and Afon Wen. There were also single-platform stations without crossing loops at Llanbedr, Talsarnau and Abererch. North of Barmouth the worst gradients were encountered in the twelve miles between Penrhyn and Afon Wen, of which more than four and a half were steeper than 1 in 100, with a maximum of 1 in 50.

Many attempts were made to encourage traffic and in 1876-7 a boost came from an unexpected quarter. It happened when Upping-ham Public School went into emergency quarantine at Borth after several boys died of typhoid. The school took over the Cambrian Hotel and twelve of the terraced houses opposite. A train of 18 trucks took 300 beds from Uppingham to Borth on 27 March 1876 and the school's heavy roller went in an LNWR truck to Bow Street, where a cricket field was laid out near the station. The boys them-selves arrived by special train on 4 April—an event recalled by J. H. Skryne who wrote a book called *Uppingham By The Sea* in 1878.

> Borth station was crowded with spectators from Aberystwyth and Borth itself, curious to watch the entry of the boys. Expectation was stimulated by the arrival of a train, which set all the crowd on tip-toe, and then swept through the station—a mere goods train. Half an hour's longer waiting and the right train drew up, and discharged Uppingham School on the remote Welsh platform.

Before they returned to Uppingham on 12 April 1877 the boys went on several excursions from Borth:

> The benevolent Cambrian railway supplies spare carriages and return tickets at single fares. Presently the train is sighted sliding down the winding incline from Langfihangel; (sic) it picks us all up—near two hundred souls, it may be—moves out into the open plain, still glittering with morning dew, and reaching Glandovey, drops half its passengers, while it carries the rest to Machynlleth and Cemmes Road.

CHAPTER 5

The Cambrian is Formed

OPPOSITION AND HELP

By carrying the coast history up to the completion of the Pwllheli line in 1867, we have overlooked much of its political history, written largely by the Cambrian which was formed only five weeks after the Aberystwyth & Welsh Coast reached Aberystwyth.

The way for the Cambrian's creation had been paved by the close alliance between the four companies which owned the lines between Whitchurch and Machynlleth and the successful operation of the Oswestry & Newtown Joint Committee. It resulted in a Bill being presented to Parliament in March 1864 to enable the Oswestry, Ellesmere & Whitchurch, the Oswestry & Newtown, the Llanidloes & Newtown and the Newtown & Machynlleth to amalgamate as the Cambrian Railways (the title took the plural from the first negotiations). The Aberystwyth & Welsh Coast was forced to withdraw from the amalgamation because it could not conform with Standing Orders.

The Bill was passed on 25 July despite strong opposition from the mighty GWR and the puny Bishop's Castle Railway, which was retaliating for the recent dismissal of four of its directors, including Whalley, from the board of the Oswestry & Newtown. The Act protected the two other big Welsh companies which were not involved in the amalgamation: the A & WC and the Mid Wales Railway, laying down that it must not do anything to take away or lessen the position of the A & WC. It was also to give the MWR full and free interchange after its opening from Llanidloes to Talyllyn. (This was then imminent and it was accomplished on 21 September.)

The MWR considered that the only effect of the Bill would concern its traffic arrangements and it was satisfied about those as it was provided that if an arbitrator found that either company was failing to provide proper facilities, then the other could use its line, stations, watering places, sidings and other necessary facilities on payment of 75 per cent of gross receipts.

The safeguards were in keeping with the Cambrian's declared future policy which was outlined in a report to the first directors' meeting by Earl Vane and George Lewis. Dated 23 July 1864, the report stated that it was now admitted that aggressive policies adopted by 'the Great Companies' had injured not only their owners but the public as well. The Cambrian's policy was based on an avowal that it was better for the company and the public that authorised lines should be used for traffic development in a way beneficial to owners. This was to be by co-operation under friendly agreements. Parliament, it pointed out, was against companies using further energies and money fighting over duplicate and unnecessary lines.

The Cambrian's Act provided for a joint board of between six and twelve directors. They held their first meeting at the company's offices in Bridge Street, Westminster, on 13 August, when Earl Vane, formerly the N & M's chairman, was elected to that office, with Captain J. W. Johns as his deputy. Other directors also came from the boards of constituent companies and George Lewis, secretary of the O & N, L & N and OE & W, was an obvious choice for secretary and general manager. George Owen, who had been engineer to most of the constituents, celebrated his appointment as engineer, by succeeding Savin as Mayor of Oswestry.

In contrast to the GWR's opposition to the infant Cambrian, the LNWR offered practical help and, on its formation day, signed a secret agreement (back-dated to 23 April) for running powers over the Cambrian in return for a 50 per cent rebate on LNWR traffic rates from Welshpool and on all through traffic, except minerals. It was to run for 99 years after which either company could give four years' notice to terminate the agreement.

A man who had a far-reaching influence not only on this agreement, but on the Cambrian's relations with the LNWR during the lean early years, was George Findlay, who had been Brassey's manager on the Shrewsbury & Hereford Railway. In 1861, Savin, who was busy constructing lines, appointed him manager of his lines as well, and in the following year Findlay became LNWR district manager for Shropshire and South Wales. This occurred after the S & H ended Brassey's contract. Findlay left Savin in 1865 to become the LNW's general goods manager, but retained a sympathy and understanding of the problems of the mid-Wales railways and this became even more valuable in keeping harmony when he began a fourteen-year term as general manager of the LNWR in 1879.

But his reign did not lead to the Cambrian getting everything it would have liked—especially running powers to Crewe. Continually it stressed the inconvenience which its passengers suffered by not being able to get to Crewe without changing. It put the point forcefully when it agreed to the LNWR making track improvements at Whitchurch station in December 1864. There was no reply from the LNWR and there was nothing the Cambrian could do but accept the snub gracefully. It was perhaps in the hope of better things to come that it agreed to the LNWR using Welshpool station from 1 January 1865.

SAVIN GOES BANKRUPT

The Cambrian's first months were satisfactory with Savin paying a proportion of his receipts and the company declaring a 5 per cent ordinary dividend for its first half-year. As the Aberystwyth & Welsh Coast amalgamated there was loose talk of a 'Great Cambrian' and much of the speculation centred on Savin as he was also working the Brecon & Merthyr and the partly-finished Carnarvonshire railways. It was also thought that the Mid Wales Railway would join in. Hopes increased as a fresh contract was arranged with Savin in January 1866 for the speedy completion of the coast line.

Such then were the pinnacles from which everything crashed when, within a month, Savin suspended all payments. The date— one of the blackest in Welsh railway history—was 5 February 1866. He was ruined by his continual acceptance of shares instead of money in his quest for power. When he gave details of his liabilities to the Cambrian two days later, he stated that he had instructed his officers at Oswestry to bank all traffic receipts, starting from the previous day.

The Cambrian was now left to complete the coast line and forced without notice to take over the working of its lines. As a first step Elijah Elias was appointed traffic manager the day after the crash and Alexander Walker took charge of rolling-stock. There were all sorts of other complications. The Cambrian claimed from Savin £7,097 7s 2d for his traffic; £5,282 6s 6d for engine hire and stores. Solicitors were instructed to take action after it was reported to the board on 26 July that he had taken no notice of several requests for payment.

The Cambrian got an Income Tax demand for £2,301 in connection with traffic Savin had handled and the company asked to pay it in instalments. It came at a time when it was already struggling to find money to meet half-yearly dividends. Board meetings to consider the question were adjourned three times within a month. The directors decided the only thing they could do was to seek a loan and a week after the crash the North & South Wales Bank was asked for a secured loan of £30,000. It took two months to reply —and then said it could advance only £23,000. It was received gratefully and shareholders were paid in May after the directors had given personal guarantees against the loan. Meanwhile, the board had to work out priorities for paying preference holders of the coast and inland sections following the A & WC amalgamation and Elias was asked to separate traffic receipts covering the original Cambrian line and the coast section.

After his failure, Savin said he was anxious to finish the coast line and the Cambrian responded by stating that it was willing to help as much as possible. Then, at a board meeting on 5 April, Savin opposed several questions concerning his position and Earl Vane asked him not to attend future meetings unless he was either invited or had matters he wanted to discuss. The chairman added that the board was placed in a painful position, but it had a duty to shareholders.

Hopes of a quick completion of the line were dogged by a failure more sensational than Savin's. It came on 10 May—'Black Friday', as it became known—with the failure of the Overend & Gurney Bank, then the world's biggest discounting house with liabilities of £11,000,000. On the Cambrian the crisis was aggravated by Savin's Receiver being unable at first to settle claims by various companies for the return of their own rolling-stock. As some of the Cambrian's was being used on the Brecon & Merthyr and other lines, the board claimed £12,102 for locomotives on B & M hire, £3,161 for others being used by the contractor on building the line, and £966 from the Denbigh, Ruthin & Corwen Railway. The claims were not settled until the end of 1867 and meanwhile a row had developed in October 1865 when the Cambrian disputed Savin's right by agreement to use its stock on lines in South Wales. Savin replied that it was only hired on a similar basis to other companies.

On 18 May 1866, Savin counterclaimed for £103,263, made up of £46,000 for work on the A & WC; £40,333 for that on the Oswestry & Newtown; £8,250 for that on the Llanidloes & Newtown; and £8,020 for that on the Oswestry, Ellesmere & Whitchurch. In discharge, the total claim was £54,159 and the Cambrian settled for £54,000 in Lloyds Bonds after Savin withdrew suits outstanding against the company.

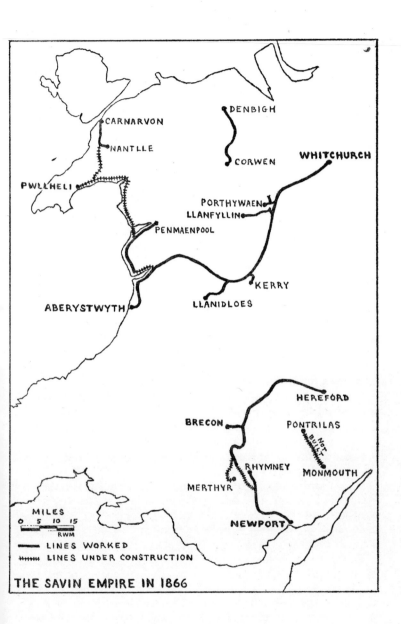

DENBIGH

CARNARVON

NANTLLE

CORWEN

WHITCHURCH

PWLLHELI

PORTHYWAEN
LLANFYLLIN

PENMAENPOOL

KERRY

ABERYSTWYTH

LLANIDLOES

HEREFORD

BRECON

PONTRILAS

NOT BUILT

RHYMNEY

MONMOUTH

MERTHYR

MILES
0 5 10 15
RWM

NEWPORT

LINES WORKED

LINES UNDER CONSTRUCTION

THE SAVIN EMPIRE IN 1866

After his failure, Savin took no further part in railway building, contenting himself with his coal mining and quarrying interests near Llanymynech. He continued to play a leading part in the civic life of Oswestry, of which he had been Mayor three years earlier. He was held in high regard and became an Alderman in 1871 and lived in the area until he died in 1889.

With the extra responsibility of working its own line, the board decided to move its headquarters nearer home and the offices were transferred from London to Oswestry station in August 1866. The financial situation was critical because two debenture holders were suing for £6,000 and in board minutes of 17 November 1866, which were struck out before being signed, it was decided to apply to the Court of Chancery 'first thing on Monday morning' for the secretary and traffic manager to be appointed as receivers for the whole of the Cambrian Railways, including the coast section. A footnote by Earl Vane said: 'No-one should know of this application until it is made in court and it must be proceeded with at once'. Further references to a receiver were again struck out before the minutes of the next board meeting on 22 November were signed. These instructed Abraham Howell, the solicitor, to guard against the threat of the appointment of a hostile receiver. If the secretary got to hear this was likely, he was to take immediate steps to have himself and the traffic manager appointed as receivers instead. Minutes struck out from the next meeting on 14 December referred to sureties for both men as receivers.

The crisis passed when a scheme for paying preference dividends was lodged in Chancery and it was agreed that an additional loan should be raised. The Court advised that this loan could be maintained by levying a rent for the use of rolling-stock.

In the middle of all the troubles there was talk of expansion and on 26 April—only about ten weeks after Savin's failure—shareholders heard preliminary details of plans to build a harbour at Porth Dinlleyn and to amalgamate with the Carnarvonshire and Nantlle Railways (with which Savin was connected). These were mentioned in a 'Great Cambrian' context. A merger was also planned with the narrow-gauge Beddgelert and Corris Railways, but in October shareholders were told this idea had been abandoned. By then, the 'Great Cambrian' concept had cooled off and the Cambrian refused overtures to join a Union of Welsh Railways, saying the time was not yet ripe. (The Beddgelert Railway was, in any event, purely a paper plan for a line from the Croesor & Portmadoc Railway. Eventually it got an Act on 6 August 1872 under the title of the North Wales Narrow Gauge Railway, the main line of which was to continue to Bettws-y-Coed. It was abandoned on 13 July 1876.)

Arrangements were made to accommodate the Manchester & Milford Railway on its arrival at Aberystwyth. It was building a single line northwards as the culmination of a scheme which arose out of the ashes of the grandiose attempts of 1845 to drive a trunk line through mid-Wales to Lancashire. By 1860, this had dwindled into a rather absurd route from Llanidloes to the Carmarthen & Cardigan Railway at Pencader and an Act was received on 23 July 1860 and another on 11 July 1861 for a branch from Devil's Bridge to Aberystwyth. When funds ran short, a third Act was obtained in 1865 by which the mountain section to Llanidloes was abandoned and the M & M's line diverted north-west to Aberystwyth from Strata Florida, which was to have been the starting point for the mountain crossing and was also the village to which the first section of the line was being built from Pencader.

The approach of the M & M settled one problem for the A & WC: what to do about building a branch to Aberystwyth Harbour. It had decided to get powers in 1863 at the same time as its Ffestiniog extension was being considered. With the collapse of that Bill, matters rested until the Aberystwyth terminal was under construction two years later. Then it was decided to support the M & M's harbour branch application, the A & WC being content with running powers. In August 1865 the companies agreed to share passenger expenses at Aberystwyth, paying for goods traffic in proportion. The M & M also agreed to pay 5 per cent interest on the cost of lines built specially for its use, but after that relations deteriorated and the next spring the Cambrian refused to let the M & M have either its own station or platforms, claiming there was no suitable land.

The M & M, which opened the first section of its single line from Pencader to Lampeter on 1 January 1866, extended to Strata Florida on 1 September and through to Aberystwyth on 12 August 1867. The harbour branch was never built.

Working agreements continued to be negotiated through the years, but they were often tender and the Cambrian played 'the senior partner' role by insisting, among other things, that the M & M should waive its right to be consulted about the appointment of station staff.

Although the M & M had to be content with a short bay platform in the Cambrian's passenger terminus, it did establish its own separate goods station at Aberystwyth.

THE GREAT WESTERN BREAKS THROUGH

The coast line had connections at several points with early narrow-gauge lines, several of them near Portmadoc. These lines, built to serve local slate quarries, included the horse-drawn Croesor Tramway, constructed without Parliamentary powers about 1863 to the same 2 ft gauge as the Festiniog, to link quarries in the Croesor valley, about seven miles away. As the A & WC drove north, the Tramway's Portmadoc section was converted into a public railway as the Croesor & Portmadoc Railway, incorporated on 5 July 1865. To reach Portmadoc Harbour it crossed the Cambrian on the level and at an angle of about 45 deg, to the east of the station. The A & WC abandoned its own plans for a Portmadoc Harbour branch when it got running powers over this narrow-gauge line at a royalty of a penny a ton. The Croesor was offered running powers into Portmadoc station if the A & WC carried traffic from there to local wharves.

Further east, the main line was also crossed on the level by the Gorsedda Tramway built, again without Parliamentary powers, about the same time as the Croesor. It ran to mines near Snowdon.

The one line with which the coast had no connection at first was the most prosperous of all—the Festiniog. This was much its senior, having been authorised by Act of 23 May 1832 and opened on 20 April 1836. The A & WC was driven underneath it near Minffordd but no connection was attempted for some years. As the A & WC had not been completed by the time the Festiniog was converting from horse to steam in 1863, the narrow-gauge locomotives were delivered by road from Carnarvon.

In the wake of the coast line opening a number of minor works were carried out, despite a 'credit squeeze' on the whole of the Cambrian. A siding was authorised at Barmouth in November 1867, at a cost of £100, and an extra platform at Glandovey Junction, costing £15, but work was ordered to be stopped on refreshment rooms at Afon Wen and Portmadoc because they had not been authorised officially. Water tanks, costing £31 6s 8d each, were ordered for Portmadoc and Llwyngwril in April 1868. In the same month a request was turned down from the Countess de Mocella for Llwyngwril station to be moved so as to give her better access to her land. She was told it would endanger the safety of the line. Further minor developments came in the autumn and on 1 September a siding was agreed for the Henddol Slate Company, provided that company paid the cost of construction and half that of having a signalman to control it. Sidings were agreed at Talsarnau and Harlech (on 26 October) and at Portmadoc, where a goods shed (£250) and engine shed (£180) were also built. A private passenger horse tramway ran for a time until about 1880 from Harlech station to the sea front.

The next development came only a fortnight after the opening of the coast line when work started on completing the Dolgelley branch from Penmaenpool, its terminus since 3 July 1865. It reopened fresh, though never serious, conflict with the GWR and to put it into perspective we must first take a look at the position east of the town. The nominally-independent companies striking west from Ruabon—the Vale of Llangollen, the Llangollen & Corwen, the Corwen & Bala and the Bala & Dolgelly—all got running powers from Dolgelley to Barmouth and Aberystwyth in the A & WC Deviation Act of 5 July 1865. As events turned out, they were premature because the progress of the promoters through the Dee valley beyond Corwen was sluggish. The first 4¾ miles of the Corwen & Bala to Llandrillo were not opened until 16 July 1866 and the next six miles to what later became Bala Lake Halt took almost two more years. But there was then only a short period between the opening of that section on 1 April 1868 and the remaining 18¼ miles to Dolgelley. They followed on 4 August. But still the running powers were not needed, for the Cambrian had not closed the gap to Penmaenpool.

To outbid the GWR, the Cambrian got a contract on 15 April 1868 to handle Dolgelley's mail, via Penmaenpool, and then set about removing the last obstacles to the completion of the branch: legal difficulties over land which had held up work for so long. They were overcome by landowners being served with notices of acquisition. By February 1869, work was well advanced and on 28 April the Cambrian decided to exercise powers under the 1865 Act to run a short distance over the Bala & Dolgelly to get access to its Dolgelley station. Shortly afterwards it had second thoughts and sought conciliatory talks with the GWR instead. The Cambrian's approach to Dolgelley was smoothed by the GWR being offered running powers to Barmouth and the branch was opened to a temporary terminus (a small wooden platform and hut) at the western end of the Bala & Dolgelly goods yard on 21 June 1869. On 1 August, Cambrian trains started using the remaining 28 ch into the permanent station. The B & D goods station opened 1 October.

The main effect of the completion was to establish a fresh link

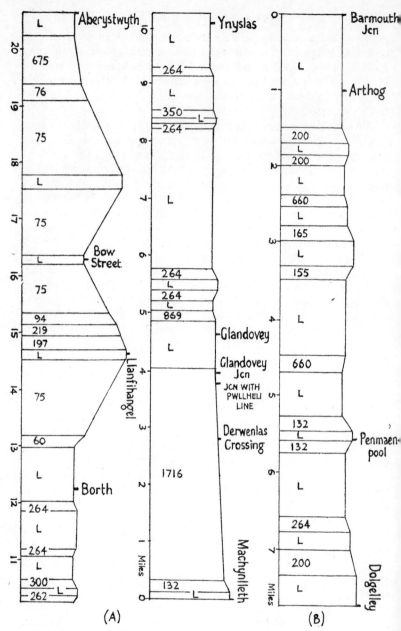

Gradient profiles: (A) Machynlleth to Aberystwyth (B) Dolgelley branch

(as an alternative to the LNWR Carnarvon line) between the coast and Merseyside, and GWR trains from Ruabon were extended to Barmouth, worked by Cambrian engines from Dolgelley, and through summer trains were introduced from Birkenhead. The next branch development was the opening of a single-platform station at Arthog on 28 March 1870, but no crossing loop was added.

A fresh agreement of 1 February 1873 consolidated relations with the GWR and the Bala & Dolgelly and under it the GWR maintained the line, but soon there was more trouble with the Cambrian and on 3 July 1874 two directors were appointed to try and come to an amicable agreement with the GWR over the Barmouth running powers. The approach failed and the dispute went to the Railway Commissioners, but the GWR still did not normally use powers beyond Dolgelley.

The GWR's initiative in driving to Dolgelley brought fair rewards. While abandoning the plan to regauge the Corris Railway as a spearhead to Aberystwyth robbed it of the chance to take most of the Cambrian's traffic between the resort and the North of England, the Dolgelley line siphoned off most of the through traffic to and from the coast north of Aberdovey away from the Whitchurch line and hence from the LNWR. The GWR increased its portion of through revenue by absorbing the Bala & Dolgelly in August 1877 and again by amalgamation with the other three small companies between Ruabon and Bala in 1896. They had, of course, all been leased and worked by the GWR from their inception. Although the Dolgelley line had no branches, there was for a time a narrow-gauge tramway which ran from Garth Sidings (three miles beyond Pen-maenpool and one-and-a-half short of Arthog) to Tyn-y-Coed quarry, south of the line.

YEARS OF STRUGGLE

In March 1867 it was decided to abandon provision of pre-preference shares for either the Coast or Inland sections, but six months later steps were taken to reduce capital to create a sounder financial footing. Shareholders appointed a committee of twelve, including Lord Powis, to assist the directors, who agreed to forego fees for a year. While the scheme was still being considered, the Cambrian went bankrupt and on 15 February 1868 Captain Robert D. Pryce, who had just become deputy chairman, was appointed as Receiver. What was known as 'The Scheme' went before the board on 31 March 1868. It had been drawn up jointly by creditors, share-holders and directors. After considering alternative proposals lodged

F

in Chancery, the board decided to include an agreement between the Coast and Inland sections. The powers were given teeth by clauses added to a Bill then before Parliament and the Act, passed on 31 July, provided that all the revenue should immediately form a common fund and that, after the deduction of working expenses, the net profit of the whole of the system was to be shared on the basis of: Coast, 35 per cent for three years followed by 37 per cent for the next four; Inland, the balance. Under the Act, the Receivership was superseded and the traffic receipts from 1 August were put into a new account of the North & South Wales Bank at Oswestry. After seven years the scheme was to be revised by arbitrators to take into account factors affecting each section.

When the plan was sent to members of the committee, it was pointed out that this was done 'having regard to the serious position of the company and of the absolute necessity of an immediate settlement of its affairs'. At the same time the Cambrian sought powers to raise extra capital of £47,300 for the Inland and £100,000 for the Coast sections.

From 1 July the board was reorganised to have ten directors: four elected by Inland interests; four by the Coast, and the other two were to be Lord Vane and Lord Powis, or their nominees. An influential group of Inland shareholders persuaded David Davies to return to represent them as a director. He immediately set about trying to reconcile the conflicting interests, although he knew that the coast section was hopelessly uneconomic, with a revenue that year of only £54,912. Years later Davies described the Cambrian's agreement to work the coast section as 'completely disastrous' as the costs totalled 88 per cent of the gross receipts. This meant that as the Cambrian received only 45 per cent of them, it amounted to £28,080 in the year under review, leaving a loss of £26,832.

A fresh crisis arose in September 1869 when landowners pressed claims for payment by threatening to retake and sell land on which the railway ran. One claim was settled for £25,000, plus legal costs and interest, and worried by the result of similar claims against other companies the Cambrian offered shares as securities, paying interest temporarily out of income. 'The Scheme' was at best an uneasy marriage and it did little to settle squabbles between the sections. The inland directors felt their more prosperous section was being saddled not only with the cost of running the coast line, but also with the cost of the final construction work, including building the Dolgelley branch.

Against this background a powerful group of shareholders

appointed a Committee of Reconstruction on 27 October 1869. It aimed at getting harmonious and effective action to improve the Cambrian as a whole, irrespective as far as possible of conflicting interests. At a board meeting on 25 November, Captain Pryce was asked by the group to resign and make way for one of their nominees. The Inland directors refused to accept the nomination and their Coast colleagues kept silent. At a shareholders' meeting on the same day there was a protest that no provision had been made for the payment of interest to general creditors, whose powers of recovery had been restricted by the Cambrian's 1868 Act. It was suggested that a fund should be started to pay creditors—as Chancery had suggested. Its income was to come from rolling-stock rent. This proposal was to emerge as one of the hottest points of conflict between the two sides.

Fresh pressure came from shareholders in February 1870 when they demanded the resignation of the whole of the board, except for the chairman and his deputy. The move was spearheaded by leaders of shareholders with Manchester interests. It failed, but the shareholders continued to be critical of the board and at a meeting on 4 March 1870 said they had no confidence in it. A little later the Inland directors got angry when the Coast's solicitor was appointed to conduct Chancery proceedings. They said this was wrong as he was also the solicitor to Savin's inspectors and had been conducting arbitration by the Coast against the Inland section! When fresh resignations were called for, Captain Pryce wrote indignantly (on 31 March) saying he was legally and morally bound to represent the interests of a substantial number of shareholders. Late the following month tension eased when the board accepted a suggestion from the Manchester interests that E. S. Bolden, who had recently become a director, should take over the general supervision of the company's affairs and receive £1,500 in lieu of directors' fees.

Besides the question of whether a hire charge should be made for rolling-stock, there was also contention (as with all railways) about whether new rolling-stock should be paid for out of capital or from revenue when this was available.

A board-room battle developed—literally—when F. A. Fynney was appointed a Coast director in place of James A. Mann. As the minutes of the first meeting attended by Fynney were being read, Mann walked in and took his seat and stated that he would not leave unless force was used. By force he meant the deputy chairman putting his hand on his shoulder! The deputy chairman refused and retired to his private room. Mann, who was kept out of the room, then left and the meeting continued. On his election, Fynney had received a majority of 3,778 votes, but he was disqualified when it was found that he was earning money from the Cambrian as an accountant.

At this period the Coast directors protested against the rent of rolling-stock—between £9,000 and £12,000 a year—being charged against the working expenses.

Yet another peace-making move came in December 1874, this time from the Cambrian's solicitors, Ashurst and Morris. They announced their intention of promoting a Bill designed to settle the differences of the two sections by taking powers to refer disputes to the Railway Commissioners. The board's reaction was one of great surprise, and members decided to oppose it in all its stages. They quickly got the support of shareholders who felt the Bill would only perpetuate the conflict between the two sections—and some protested against the Cambrian having to spend money on opposing its own Bill!

Another factor in inter-section relations was the Cambrian's relationship as a whole with the LNWR. On the one hand the Cambrian had to try and persuade the LNWR to provide better and quicker services and connections from London and other towns. On the other hand it had to negotiate delicately over rebates on traffic which was handled *via* Afon Wen and Welshpool. Both were often in bitter dispute, and relations were further strained when the Cambrian took a claim for a £9,000 rebate on Welshpool traffic to arbitration in June 1866 after the LNWR had continually refused to pay. At the same time it admitted the GWR to Welshpool on the same terms as the LNWR. While the Coast directors tried to squeeze every penny out of the LNWR over Afon Wen rebates to swell their coffers (and hence their prestige in the eyes of their Inland colleagues), the Inland directors led by the chairman, Earl Vane (who had now become Lord Londonderry on the death of his father), were constantly appealing for restraint. This policy seems to have paid dividends in maintaining satisfactory relations with the LNWR although the Cambrian again went to arbitration in 1876 when, on 16 March, the verdict was given in its favour.

During the Cambrian's struggling years, several minor lines were developed or planned around it. The healthiest (which were still terribly weak) were two standard-gauge lines built as a result of the opening of the main line. Both were independently owned and worked and the first, the Mawddwy Railway, opened on 1 October 1867 to passengers and goods. It provided limited slate traffic from local quarries which the Cambrian worked forward to Aberdovey Harbour for shipment. During the slate boom as the industrial towns and cities of Britain were hastily built, slate traffic off the Talyllyn and Corris Railways was also shipped from Aberdovey.

The second line was the Van Railway, opened to goods only on 14 August 1871. While some lead traffic developed from the Van mines, the Van's main value to the Cambrian was as a source of fine track ballast with a weed-killing capacity.

Both lines were destined to join the Cambrian in later years. Of far greater importance was the Nantmawr branch which came earlier under the Cambrian's control.

Although it worked the line from 1881, the Cambrian remained in command of the branch only through adoption. To trace its ancestry we must go back to a scheme which came, completely independently, in the wake of the West Midland plan to reach the coast. It was called the West Shropshire Mineral Railway and was authorised on 29 July 1862 to run from Westbury, on the recently-completed Shrewsbury-Welshpool line, to Llanymynech—a distance of 13¾ miles. It was promoted by R. S. France, Secretary of the Mid Wales Railway, builder of the Mawddwy Railway and the owner of limestone quarries at Llanymynech. His scheme lay dormant for two years until, on 30 June 1864, it got powers to change its name to the Shrewsbury & North Wales Railway and build several new lines. Its starting point was changed from Westbury to Redhill, three miles south of Shrewsbury, with a branch to tap mineral resources in the Briedden Hills, rising from the Shropshire plain. It was to be extended from Llanymynech to Llanyblodwell and go on from there with another line to Llangynog. There were also plans for lines from Llanyblodwell to Oswestry, the Nantmawr lime kilns and Porthywaen; a junction with the Llanfyllin branch, and a branch from Llanymynech to the Shropshire Union Canal about 300 yd east of the Oswestry & Newtown bridge across it.

Five years were allowed for completion and there were to be no further extensions without the agreement of the O & N, which was to retain running powers over the main stem of the Shrewsbury & North Wales and also have them between Llanyblodwell and Porthywaen and on the canal branch, and have part use of the line to the kilns. There was no stipulation about running powers to Llangynog or from Llanyblodwell to Oswestry.

The line was routed to cross the O & N on the level south of Llanymynech and continue westwards for three-quarters of a mile

before turning north to the quarries after crossing above the Llanfyllin branch. This was the route first favoured by the West
Midland. If necessary, Llanymynech station was to be extended at
s & nw expense by driving another arch through the turnpike road
bridge over it.

Once the scheme got under way it quickly attracted the authorities at King's Cross and Stoke-on-Trent, who dreamed of the Great
Northern and the North Staffordshire Railways serving the Welsh
coast. As a first step they supported two connecting lines to the
s & nw—the Stafford & Uttoxeter of 1862 and the Shrewsbury &
Potteries Junction Railway which was to close the gap between
Shrewsbury and Market Drayton. The s & nw amalgamated with the
Shrewsbury & Potteries to emerge, on 16 July 1866, as the more
renowned Potteries, Shrewsbury & North Wales Railway. It was
opened from Shrewsbury (Abbey Foregate) to Nantmawr less than a
month later: on 13 August. Although work had started on the
Shrewsbury-Market Drayton section, it was killed by the financial
crisis of that year and as a result the GNR's dreams of reaching the
Welsh coast ebbed gently away in a quarry at Nantmawr, so far
from the sea.

The Nantmawr line became a rival to the traffic of the struggling
Cambrian, yet relations were friendly and, as soon as the PS & NW
opened, through coaches were run from Shrewsbury to Oswestry
on Saturdays. There were also weekend excursions from Shrewsbury
to Aberystwyth. But traffic was terribly light (it was goods only on
the Nantmawr branch) and all services stopped on 21 December
1866 and did not resume for two years. Passenger trains did not run
to Llanyblodwell on the Nantmawr line until 18 April 1870. The line
fell into a state of decay and it was closed by the Board of Trade
on 22 June 1880 and the company went into liquidation. On the day
of close-down R. S. France asked the Cambrian to take over the
Nantmawr quarry traffic and to consider the possibility of rerouting
it *via* Buttington to the Lilleshall Iron Works near Wellington. The
Cambrian made a temporary arrangement with the PS & NW on
28 January 1881 which led to it working traffic over the branch
(3 m 70 ch from Llanymynech to the quarries) for two years.
Working began on 1 June 1881 at a royalty of threepence a ton,
reduced by a penny on 1 January 1886.

The rest of the 'Potts' rotted slowly away during the eighties
despite several efforts by yet another company, the Shropshire
Railways, to reopen it. When it did finally manage to get an Act on
7 August 1888 to acquire the line it was estimated that £3,000 was

needed to recondition the Nantmawr branch alone. The Cambrian got running powers over the whole system; the Shropshire was given access to Oswestry in return. Some work was done but the new company was unable to reopen the Llanymynech-Shrewsbury stem.

CHAPTER 6

Under Attack and Bankrupt Again

'STAB IN THE DARK'

The internal (and external) board squabbles ended in 1878 when it was finally realised that 'The Scheme' was not working. It was decided to revert to the constitution laid down in the 1865 Amalgamation Act and combined accounts were reintroduced for the Coast and Inland sections from 1 January 1879 and a new board was elected the following month. The new union was quickly under attack and its fiercest critic was David Davies. The first hint of discord passed undetected at a shareholders' meeting on 30 August 1878 when he criticised the condition of the track. As he was a director, nobody sensed trouble when he complained that part of the track had been badly constructed—adding, amid laughter, that it was not the part which he had made. He went on to claim that working expenses would be cut only when new steel rails were laid.

The storm broke early in 1879 when Davies, who was not seeking re-election to the board, sent a pamphlet called *Cambrian Railways Workshops* to directors and shareholders. Despite its innocent title, it made a wide ranging attack on the various activities of the company. Davies claimed, for instance, that an excessive number of locomotives were under repair at Oswestry. He also alleged that a fellow-director, S. H. Hadley, had stated that he would like to see Oswestry Works burned down and new ones built at Aberystwyth. Finance was also criticised and Davies followed up his pamphlet at the half-yearly shareholders' meeting a few days later. This time he made a personal attack on the board and demanded the setting-up of a committee of inquiry into the company. Lord Londonderry described it as 'a stab in the dark', and regretted, as did others, that Davies had not consulted the directors with whom he had been associated for so long before making it. Davies claimed the track was very nearly a wreck and appealed for a Board of Trade inspection. He claimed that it was not safe and said he would not be surprised to see the railway sprinkled with human blood very shortly. In his pamphlet, Davies had written that 'the men are patching up the line in every direction with old rails, often not lasting a week after they are put in'. He alleged that it took up nearly all their time just to do repairs and that the engineer, George Owen, had been told there was no money to pay for new rails. Owen denied this and the company also had some pretty conclusive facts which made Davies look silly. It retorted that there had not been an accident due to bad track for ten years. Regarding locomotive repairs, while it was true that at the end of 1878 there was an unusual number in works, thirteen or fifteen out of forty-nine,* this was mainly due to the severe winter. About forty wagons needed renewal, but the cost could be kept to under £1,650. There was no shortage of them because the number in use was sufficient to meet all the traffic, due to the depressed state of trade.

Reports by chief officers showed that, despite all its difficulties, the company was not doing badly. Between 1869 and 1878 expenditure compared favourably with other railways in England and Scotland. The most the Cambrian spent on track was £46,219 in 1877—and that included £3,328 for repairs after a January storm. The life of rails was given as about eleven years on single lines, fifteen on double. In ten years repairs to engines, carriages and wagons totalled £185,766. Accident compensation was only £1,667.

After his outburst Davies left the meeting and the board and severed his connection with the Cambrian for ever. The meeting ended with further rebuttals of Davies' complaints, but on 3 March 1879 Davies wrote from his home at Llandinam to Lord Londonderry to clarify a few points raised at the meeting. After reviewing the Inland and Coast finances he went on to say that he thought the Kerry and Llanfyllin branches were both making a loss while the Oswestry, Ellesmere & Whitchurch was probably making a profit of £8,000 a year. He pointed out that the whole system, which then stretched 178 miles, had a capital of £4,401,153, or £24,275 a mile. After about fifteen years of working the lines the Cambrian had never been able to pay dividends on more than £1,600,000. Maintenance had cost £1,100,000, leaving a capital of £2,801,153 on which no dividend had ever been paid. It had to be remembered, Davies contended, that, even without renewing bridges, the permanent way needed at least £80,000 to put it in good working order.

'Looking at these startling facts, I took it for granted that all to

---

* Actually 46 engines were in stock at the end of 1878

whom I addressed my statement would at once understand what I meant by saying "there is £2,400,000 of capital not worth the paper it is written upon".'

Davies asked the chairman to give him some explanation which he could publish showing how a large proportion of stock which he had called valueless was created and issued to pay him during construction and how he was responsible, as the chairman's words seemed to imply, for the fact that he had lived in affluence while there were widows and orphans in Lancashire in very reduced circumstances because husbands and fathers invested money in that stock on the faith of its bona fides.

Lord Londonderry's reply was terse. It began by telling Davies: 'Had you not left the room you would probably have heard the few remarks which I made in reply to the violent personal speech which you saw fit to make'. He again accused Davies of grossly maligning the board and officers 'for no reason I could possibly fathom'. He continued: 'I must decline, with the approval of the Board, to enter into any controversy with you. Your accusations being too *general* I cannot *individually* repel them further. May I express a hope that in time you may feel a pang of regret that you treated your old colleagues in the way you have done.'

Davies never did so and his spite in later years took a more petty form when he always rebooked his through journeys at Welshpool to deprive the Cambrian of its half-share of LNWR bookings from there.

The row with Davies had no lasting effect; neither did it help to solve some of the Cambrian's pressing problems which stemmed from the shortage of money. The Cambrian felt more keenly than buoyant companies the continued general depression in trade and agriculture at this period. Economies were made whenever possible and in 1880 main-line re-laying was cut from twenty-one to seventeen miles.

The depression of the slate industry and heavy failures in the flannel trade of Newtown were blamed for the continued traffic decline in 1883 and staff were ordered by the board to exercise the utmost economy, which was needed until the end of the year, 'consistent with safety and efficiency'. The following year brought no respite to the depression and receipts for the first half were £81,147 against expenditure of £48,912. It represented a net revenue increase of only £132. Economies were reflected in expenditure dropping by £304.

Crisis was reached again when receipts failed to cover debenture interests and the company's bankers started an action. It resulted in the Cambrian being placed in the hands of the Court of Chancery on 12 July 1884. The directors became managers and John Conacher, who had been secretary since 1882, was appointed as receiver.

'TRADERS LEAVING WALES . . .'

While he was a fiery man who quickly clashed with some of the staff, Conacher now set about steering the company on to a firm footing in a way which was destined to make him one of the ablest officers ever associated with it.

He took office at a time when the Cambrian, besides being in Chancery, was also under heavy attack from critics. They included *The Railway News* which stated on 23 August that the Cambrian could not hope to withdraw from Chancery until it had wiped out at least half of its capital—particularly as revenue was practically stagnant and there was little or no prospect of an improvement for at least five years. The magazine claimed that the directors would be unwise to depend on revenue to rescue them: the need was for reorganisation.

At the shareholders' summer meeting one of them, G. B. Bryan of Harlech, alleged that some traders were languishing or leaving Wales because of the company's excessively high goods charges. Another complaint was that, although the Cambrian was only 178 miles long, it had eight directors, each costing £1,000 a year. Lord Londonderry replied that they were not allowed to have less than six and it was not excessive to have two more. He himself did not get a fee. Other shareholders rallied to the company's support and said public criticisms not only gave it a bad name, but lost it traffic. There were companies in England quite as bad, if not worse. One man pointed out that he had been a passenger on a GWR express delayed for three-quarters of an hour. If that had happened on the Cambrian they would never have heard the last of it. As long as it was on the Great Western, no notice was taken.

To put the company back on its feet, what was called the '1885 Scheme' was drawn up to reorganise finances. It provided for the seventy stocks to be consolidated into ten and the capital, including loans, became £5,834,000. The scheme was filed in Chancery on 18 February 1885—only seven months after bankruptcy—and invoked on 14 July. As it was accepted by creditors, it overcame the Cambrian's bankruptcy and the company was discharged.

Almost simultaneously, an improvement in fortunes came from

another quarter as the general depression, which had been affecting trade throughout most of Britain, began to ease. Passenger receipts for the last half of 1884 picked up by £1,556, although goods traffic remained poor. Meanwhile the Cambrian was slowly completing the job of modernisation which was to lift it out of its slough. In terms of track re-laying, it meant that 91 miles had been replaced with steel rails by 1883 and, by 1885, only ten miles of 'iron road' remained on the main line; 12¾ on the coast.

Such progress did not silence every critic and, at the shareholders' winter meeting in 1885, G. B. Bryan returned to the attack. He claimed that in its twenty-one-year existence the Cambrian had been going from bad to worse. Instead of trying to attract revenue by development, it had stagnated.

But his criticism was not borne out by receipts, which increased by £2,000 in 1886—and that at a time when 140 vessels were lying at Portmadoc waiting for an improvement in the slate trade. The following year brought a rise of £1,019 in passenger receipts even though, it was claimed, a general election upset the plans of summer travellers.

There were a number of significant board changes at this period. Lord Londonderry died in 1884 and was succeeded by Captain Pryce, his deputy for sixteen years and his colleague on the boards of the Newtown & Machynlleth and the Aberystwyth & Welsh Coast. To represent the Londonderry family, Lord Herbert Vane-Tempest joined the board. Other new directors were Arthur Charles Humphreys-Owen of Glansevern and John (later Sir John) Maclure, MP for Stretford and a director of the Manchester, Sheffield & Lincolnshire. With Conacher, Humphreys-Owen drew up the '1885 Scheme' soon after joining the board. Captain Pryce died in 1886 after only two years in the chair which was now taken by James Frederick Buckley, who was to reign until 1900.

THE ACHING LIMB

There were three main facets to the development of the coast. All began with the coming of the railway. And all were failures. There was a burst of early development by Savin, brought to an abrupt and total end by his crash. There were other attempts to develop ports and resorts and to introduce steamer services—coastal, Irish and American. As most of the local coasting trade was badly hit by the creation of the line, it was ironic that it should try and apply artificial respiration to its dead victim; poetic justice that it

£10 o Wobr

Yn gymaint ag i ryw berson neu bersonau maleis-ddrwg prydnawn Dydd Mawrth, yr 16eg cyfisol, osod dau *sleeper* ar draws llinell y Cambrian Railways, yn agos i Orsaf Llanfihangel.

Rhoddir Rhybydd drwy hyn, y telir y Wobr uchod i unrhyw berson, pa un bynag a fyddo yn gyfranog ai peidio, yr hwn a roddo hyspysrwydd a all arwain i ddaliad a chondemniad y troseddwr neu y troseddwyr a'r ymofyniad a'r hwn y mae ei enw isod.

GEO.LEWIS,
Ysgrifenydd,
Cambrian Railways Co.

Croesoswallt, Ion. 20, 1872.

£10 REWARD

Whereas, some evil disposed person or persons did on the evening of Tuesday, the 16th inst., place two sleepers across the line of the Cambrian Railways, near to Llanfihangel Station.

Notice is hereby given that the above Reward will be paid to any person whether an accomplice or not, who will give information which may lead to the apprehension or conviction of the offender or offenders, on application to the undersigned.

GEO. LEWIS,
Secretary,
Cambrian Railways Co.

Oswestry, Jan. 20, 1872.

failed. In the years before the track was laid shipping services were important. Aberystwyth was enjoying the reputation as the principal port on the whole of the coast of West Wales, more important than Carnarvon or Portmadoc. It had weekly sailings to both Liverpool and Bristol, but the railway soon put an end to those.

Yet the immediate development associated with the line's arrival was keyed to other things: attracting not only holidaymakers, but also residents who would use the trains regularly throughout the year. Schemes got off to a festive start as crowds which welcomed the first train to Aberystwyth walked down to the shore to watch the first pile driven to start a new pier. At Borth the event was marked differently. It was by the completion of a row of terraced boarding houses flanking the station approach which Savin had built as the nucleus of a new resort. They at least gave Borth an air of distinction for only a few years before guide-books were calling it a 'wretched-looking fishing village'.

Plans which the A & WC had for building and running its own hotels at the main stations were quashed by Parliament in 1864 and never revived. Savin, however, was not deterred from launching projects at Aberystwyth. He got hold of a large house on the sea front, designed by John Nash, and spared no expense to make it a first-class hotel, even though the resort already had, according to guide-books, two good hotels and 'abounded in lodging houses'. The conversion of The Castle, as the hotel was to be called, was done quickly, with over 500 men working on it, to outstrip the building of the rival Queen's Hotel, and it opened in June 1865. A week's board and lodging was offered free, conditional upon the purchase of a return from Euston, but the offer did not tempt the rich—and no-one else could afford it. Following Savin's failure, The Castle was put up for sale in November 1866. The only offer of £5,000 was refused by the Receiver and the hotel was not sold until 1872 when it was bought as the nucleus for the University College of Wales. The price paid was £10,000—one-eighth of its cost. It opened later the same year with twenty-six students.

The men who worked on hotels at Borth and Aberystwyth got cheap rail travel but as work lagged the Cambrian decided on 6 April 1866, during the crisis after Savin's crash, that they must pay normal third-class fares.

From time to time modest developments were projected. In the Aberdovey Improvements Act of 1883 the opportunity was taken to get powers to buy land at Aberech for hotels and refreshment rooms. Although the project was small in concept involving no more than £20,000 in capital it had one novel feature: facility to build a savings bank. Just over a year later the Cambrian was bankrupt!

One of its many troubles stemmed from something which Savin and the early promoters had already failed to grasp: the terrible handicap which Cardigan Bay suffers by being out on a geographical limb much farther than other coasts from the main centres of population.

Aberystwyth is 140 rail miles from Manchester; Llandudno under 80. The Cambrian limb was stretched even more in the Lleyn Peninsula, which is several miles nearer London *via* Chester than through Welshpool. Besides slow journey times, holidaymakers also had to consider higher fares for longer distances when thinking of going to Cardigan Bay.

So much for land development. Turning to that for shipping we find that the first proposals for launching Irish services which were made by an established railway company in mid-Wales (as opposed to the much earlier plans of Brunel and other promoters) was put to Parliament by the Aberystwyth & Welsh Coast Railway in a Bill of 1864. It planned a terminal at Aberdovey, which it claimed could be made cheaply into a large and safe harbour, while at the same time seeking to start a service from Porth Dinlleyn. The Bill was strongly opposed by the London shipowners and merchant shippers in Glasgow, Leith, Liverpool and London. It was withdrawn before it was due for consideration when the A & WC realised that at that time Parliament was not disposed to allowing railway companies to become steamboat owners.

But soon afterwards Parliament's attitude changed and, after other railway companies had obtained shipping powers, the A & WC presented a revised Bill to run a service from Aberystwyth and Aberdovey to Waterford and Wexford. While the application was being made the Waterford & Kilkenny Railway sought the help of the A & WC because rival Irish railways in league with the LNWR were diverting traffic from parts of Southern Ireland to the Holyhead route. The A & WC replied that until it got its own powers it could not help—but anything the Irish company could do to prevent the diversion meanwhile would be welcome.

The A & WC got its Bill through the committee stage in the spring of 1865, but it was thrown out by the Lords in June. Matters then rested for some years, but in 1880 there were discussions with the Manchester & Milford about inaugurating a company to start a service between Aberdovey and America. Nothing came of this idea, but the gentle revival of trade about this time brought other developments. New rates for Aberdovey Harbour traffic were fixed on 26 November 1881. Foreign-going vessels were charged three-pence a ton if they landed cargo on the pier, landing-stage or wharf; a penny less if they discharged cargo on the shore. Two years later —on 29 June 1883—the Cambrian received powers to improve the harbour by building another pier and embankment, costing about £2,000, and carrying out other works. The cost was to be met out of a special issue of 20,000 'Pier' stock on which shareholders were to be entitled to dividends only on tolls, rates and charges. They were not to be paid out of Cambrian revenue or receipts. The necessary land was bought the same year and an independent company—the Aberdovey & Waterford Steam Shipping Company— started a passenger service of nine sailings a month with two paddle steamers—*Liverpool* and *Cambria*.

Aberdovey Pier was widened in 1885-86, mainly to handle these steamers and 'foreign' vessels. At this time Aberdovey was handling nearly all the slate traffic from the Talyllyn, Corris and Mawddwy railways. The Cambrian was also importing many of its materials, including the majority of its timber sleepers, through the port.

The two steamers were not the first run in conjunction with the mid-Wales railways: a small paddle steamer called *Elizabeth* was used to ferry materials and rolling-stock across the Dovey estuary from Ynyslas to Aberdovey from 1862 until August 1867. Passengers were carried from November 1863 and the sailings con-nected with trains on both sides of the estuary until the Glandovey deviation was opened. The *Elizabeth* remained in Cambrian stock and when repairs were needed in 1868 the locomotive superin-tendent was authorised to carry them out, provided they did not cost more than £50. The steamer was sold—to a Mr Green—in December 1869.

When the coast line was finally opened, its northern terminus was still half a mile short of Pwllheli town and no start had been made on the extension authorised in 1862 to Porth Dinlleyn. Apart from the chronic shortage of money, the Cambrian realised—as the A & WC had done earlier—that the Irish trade, although it was developing all the time, was being handled with ease *via* Holyhead, Liverpool and other ports. Nothing was done by the A & WC to revive the extension up to amalgamation with the Cambrian which, on 26 April 1866 while still smarting under the effects of Savin's failure, decided to get powers to subscribe to a harbour at Porth Dinlleyn. But it then let matters rest for six years until it planned

LOCOMOTIVES—PASSENGER

(19) 'Albion' 2—4—0 No. 53 about 1888, modified by Aston with cab, vacuum brakes, solid splashers and new chimney

(20) Oswestry & Newtown Railway 2—4—0 'Mazeppa' as built in 1863

(21) 'Volunteer' 0—4—2 No. 5, as modified in July 1888 with vacuum brake, cab, 16 in cylinders and Aston chimney

LOCOMOTIVES—MID WALES RAILWAY

(22) *Kitson 0—4—2 with cab added and renumbered 24 by the Cambrian*

(23) *Sharp, Stewart 0—6—0 No. 9, as Cambrian No. 48, about 1898*

a revival of the scheme under a decision taken on 21 August 1874. Landowners were to be asked to accept agricultural, rather than development, value for their land. Four months later the plan was torn apart by boardroom strife between the Coast and Inland directors, with many feeling the time was not ripe for any further action. They had their way and nothing more was heard of the plan until 29 September 1876 when yet another revival was planned, this time for both a railway and a pier. Nothing happened and when the matter was raised in 1883 the embarrassed Cambrian board refused to even investigate it again.

Matters were taken away from the Cambrian by the incorporation of the Porth Dinlleyn Railway Company on 7 August 1884. It was to have a capital of £120,000 backed by loans of £40,000 and it was to have five years to build the 9¼-mile route from Pwllheli. The Cambrian regarded the new company as friendly, but there were shareholders who feared that by leaving the line to be built by another company the Cambrian would lose valuable Irish traffic which it so badly needed. The chairman told shareholders it would have been difficult for the company to have raised the capital, but it did take a bigger stake in the new company when it made an agreement, dated 26 January 1887, to work the line for 50 per cent of gross receipts, provided it was built to its own satisfaction and within the time limit. It also got power to appoint two directors. It never exercised this power, mainly because the only thing which the Porth Dinlleyn Company ever did was to get orders for the extension of building time.

The Cambrian was hardly more successful in gaining anything from its relations with feeder lines built, or projected, along the coast. The most prosperous was the Festiniog, and the Cambrian's arrival did nothing to break its monopoly on slate traffic from the quarries around Festiniog to Portmadoc. But relations did become closer when the building of exchange sidings at Minffordd was agreed on 14 October 1870. They were designed jointly by the Cambrian's engineer, Owen, and the Festiniog's, C. E. Spooner, and constructed on split levels.

Minffordd Junction station was built about the same time and appeared in both timetables in summer 1872. This summer also marked the incorporation of a new narrow-gauge company and on 21 June the Cambrian approved the formation of the Gorsedda Junction & Portmadoc Railway, which also planned a branch into the hills at Blaen-y-Pennant. The company was formed to take over the old Gorsedda tramway and was regularised by an Act of 25 July.

G

This provided that it should join the Croesor & Portmadoc Railway just north of the Cambrian crossing and use it jointly. The line was rebuilt in 1875 and the Gorsedda and Croesor trans-shipped some slate traffic to the Cambrian north of the crossing. Traffic was always light and when the Gorsedda could not pay its bills the Cambrian asked for a Receiver to be appointed on 23 January 1883.

A branch just west of Portmadoc to a quarry on the Wern Rock included the use of mixed-gauge track. The narrow gauge from the branch ran along the south side of Portmadoc station to connect with the Croesor and Gorsedda lines. In 1879 the Croesor & Portmadoc Railway changed its title to the Croesor & Beddgelert Tram Railway Company. It also got powers for a four-mile branch to Beddgelert in an Act backed by the traffic-hungry Cambrian, but the scheme was not proceeded with through lack of money.

A more promising feeder line would have been provided if the Merionethshire Railway had been built. It was incorporated on 20 June 1871 to develop a 2 ft line from Llan Festiniog (the southern terminus of the same-gauge Festiniog & Blaenau, which had opened three years before) to the Cambrian at Llandecwyn, just north of Talsarnau. It would have followed a circuitous and steeply-graded route of ten miles and linked up at Maentwrog with the proposed Bala & Festiniog Railway, with part of the route mixed gauge. The Cambrian backed the Merionethshire and on 14 July 1871 prepared a working arrangement for traffic to and from Portmadoc. Gross returns on traffic between Blaenau and Portmadoc were to be divided by mileage; the Cambrian's being calculated as four miles into Portmadoc station. There was to be a junction with the Beddgelert and Croesor railways and if they thought a signalman necessary he was to be paid by the Merioneth, which was also to maintain its line. The Cambrian was to have charge of junction signals with the coast line.

Finally, the agreement was not to prejudice any of the Cambrian's rights at Portmadoc Harbour. Although the Merioneth's chairman was Samuel Holland, a powerful quarry owner who was also chairman of the Festiniog & Blaenau and a director of the Bala & Festiniog, the plan failed. Money was not forthcoming and all that the Merionethshire ever did was to get powers for extension of time for completion. Even the opening of the Bala & Festiniog to Llan Festiniog on 1 November 1882 failed to revive hopes and the Merionethshire powers lapsed finally on 29 June 1885. The next year the Festiniog & Blaenau was converted to standard gauge and that proved sufficient for local traffic needs. No railway was ever

built over the wild and lonely terrain which the Merionethshire set
out to tame. Battle honours in the area finally went to the GWR
which by working the Blaenau & Bala lines took much of the slate
traffic which had previously been trans-shipped to the Cambrian at
Minffordd.

THE WELSH RAILWAY UNION

Contemporary with the opening and development of the coast
agitation was growing inland in support of a scheme which looked
far more promising: the development of a north-south route to
rival the lucrative Shrewsbury & Hereford line between South Wales
and Merseyside, two of Britain's fastest-growing industrial areas.

A suggestion for a Committee of Welsh Railways, including the
Cambrian, Brecon & Merthyr, Mid Wales and Potteries, Shrewsbury
& North Wales railways, was first put forward in December 1865.
The Cambrian refused to entertain the idea—and gave a similar cold
reception to a modified scheme formulated a year later to embrace
in addition the independent railways between Wrexham and
Birkenhead.

Among the most active of the Union promoters were Benjamin
Piercy and Henry Robertson and they developed a group of lines in
North Wales which finally made the Union a reality. Piercy had
engineered most of the Cambrian constituents; Robertson had been
engineer to the Shrewsbury & Chester and North Wales Mineral
railways. Both men had colliery interests in the Wrexham area and
Robertson was to be chairman of two of the nominally independent
lines in the Dee valley—the Vale of Llangollen and the Llangollen
& Corwen. The first of the North Wales lines which forged into the
Union was the Buckley Railway, authorised on 14 June 1860. It was
to convert an old tramroad from Connah's Quay and extend it five
miles to Buckley. The line was opened on 7 June 1862. The second
and biggest line had been proposed a year earlier as the Whitchurch,
Wrexham, Mold & Connah's Quay Railway from Buckley to the
Oswestry, Ellesmere & Whitchurch at Bettisfield. It was to have
running powers over the OE & W and also the Chester & Mold, Mold
& Denbigh, Vale of Clwyd and Buckley railways. Rival schemes
promoted at the same time included a GWR branch from Wrexham
to Mold and to Buckley, and the OE & W line from Ellesmere to
Ffrith. Only the twelve-and-a-half miles from Wrexham to Buckley
were authorised on 7 August 1862. The line was opened as the
Wrexham, Mold & Connah's Quay Railway on 1 May 1866. Powers
for the line from Wrexham to Bettisfield were obtained on 25 July

1864 and a three-year extension of time was obtained on 18 August 1867, but nothing was done because of lack of money and powers lapsed in 1870.

Meanwhile, in Cheshire, the Hoylake Railway had been authorised on 28 July 1863 to build a line (among others) five-and-a-quarter miles to Birkenhead docks and this opened on 2 July 1866. The next year the final link in the proposed Wales-Birkenhead route was authorised. It was a joint Hoylake and WM & CQ venture from Bidston to Connah's Quay with a tunnel under the Dee. When it failed to materialise for lack of money, the Cambrian turned down, almost out of hand, a proposal for it to join the Union. Although it felt the time was not ripe, it did have a number of ties with the WM & CQ, of which Robert Piercy was appointed resident engineer on 10 July 1866. George Lewis was the company's first secretary until he left on 9 September 1867—about the time Robert Piercy became manager. His term of office was short and he left in April of the following year. Then, when Benjamin Piercy left the WM & CQ on 19 October 1868, George Owen became engineer for a year. The Buckley Railway was absorbed by the WM & CQ on 30 June 1873— the year of another abortive scheme to cross the Dee.

Things got moving again in 1881 when Benjamin Piercy returned to Wrexham after a number of years abroad and became the largest shareholder in the WM & CQ. The first thing he did was to get an Act for a half-mile extension from the existing terminus alongside the GWR station at Wrexham to a new one in the centre of the town and this was authorised in 1882. With Robertson, Piercy now set about crossing the Dee and got the support of the Manchester, Sheffield & Lincolnshire Railway, which had reached Chester as part owner of the Cheshire Lines Railway on 2 November 1874. They encouraged the MS & L to bridge the Dee to get a million tons of coal a year from pits near Wrexham to the Cheshire salt mines. The bridge, which included a swinging span of 287 ft—then the world's largest—was officially opened on 3 August 1889.

The object of the WM & CQ's extension to Wrexham Central became apparent towards the end of 1884 with the announcement of plans for building a new line from Wrexham, not to Bettisfield, but to Ellesmere. The Wrexham & Ellesmere Railway was duly incorporated on 31 July 1885. The Manchester, Sheffield & Lincolnshire chairman, Sir Edward Watkin, saw the branch as a spearhead for a drive into Wales. He suggested that the GWR should finance it jointly with the Cambrian, WM & CQ and his own company, but with its position in Wrexham strategically secure the GWR declined. The

MS & L then paid £50,000 towards the £180,000 needed, with the Cambrian and WM & CQ as the other main subscribers. With this capital and £50,000 in loans the Wrexham & Ellesmere was incorporated. The first chairman was George Kenyon MP of Whitchurch, the eldest son of Lord Kenyon, who was a Cambrian director.

For several years nothing was done towards starting construction and an extension of time had to be obtained in 1888. But the prospect of the W & E opening in the future kept alive the idea of a Union. Initially, the Mid Wales Railway was seen as the longest link in it but the 1888 working agreement with the Cambrian gave this company potentially the lion's share.

The vision of heavy traffic flowing to and from South Wales was cherished by the mid-Wales promoters from the early days. Now we must tell the story of how that turned out to be little more than a spectre.

CHAPTER 7

A Rich Vision

THE MID WALES RAILWAY

For a line of only about fifty miles and a single route; for a line which ran through some of the loneliest—if enchanting—countryside in Britain; for a line which never reached a town of any size, the history of the Mid Wales Railway is most complex. Among its significant aspects were a whole series of early squabbles to get it built at all, followed by a complete change of direction and a battle with several companies to get access to Brecon. All events were, in turn, bound up with relations with other companies. In the early stages it was other Welsh companies which were the main foes of the Mid Wales; later it was the giants which, by one route or another, sapped away traffic, potential and actual.

It all began when, as the Montgomeryshire promoters were busy extending their lines to the north and west in the spring of 1858, a development in remote Carmarthenshire sparked off a desire for them to get access to the rapidly-growing parts of South Wales. Desire quickly crystallised into necessity as other companies were equally eager to exploit the route opened up by the completion of the Vale of Towy Railway from Llandeilo to Llandovery on 1 April 1858, especially as it had direct connections to Llanelly. At once the Shrewsbury & Hereford Railway interests, strongly supported by the LNWR, planned to exploit the spearhead of the Knighton Railway. This was poised for an extension to Llandovery under the title of the Central Wales Railway.

The Montgomeryshire interests, who felt bound to fight the S & H drive, claimed that a through line to Llandovery would be invaluable to them and they felt they could best serve the area by extending the Llanidloes & Newtown for 45 miles to the town. Money was again the stumbling block and, although the Oswestry & Newtown rejected an overture for help in October 1858, plans went ahead. A provisional board was formed and the company entitled The Manchester, Liverpool, Swansea & Milford Haven Junction Railway.

Plans for the proposed route were deposited by Benjamin Piercy as engineer of the L & N. It was to run from Llanidloes and through the Wye valley for fifteen miles *via* Newbridge and Rhayader to Builth. Here it was to turn south-west towards the village of Llanwrtyd—celebrated like Builth for its mineral springs—and then along the valley of the River Bran to Llandovery. The maximum gradient was to be 1 in 60 and the sharpest curve one with a radius of 30 ch—with the exception of one of 24 ch at Rhayader.

'Upon such a line,' commented the *Shrewsbury Journal*, 'express trains at the highest speeds reached can be run with the greatest ease and perfect security.'

The new company sought to tie together the loose ends of the original Manchester & Milford Railway, born so grandiosely during the Railway Mania and killed with almost equally dramatic flourish soon afterwards. Since then a rail link continued to be slowly forged in the general direction of both places, but it was being created incidentally as a result of companies building lines to serve places en route. By 1859 lines stretched from Manchester, through Crewe and Shrewsbury, to Llanidloes, allowing for the imminent completion of the Oswestry & Newtown. From Milford there was a line to Llandovery (except between Llandeilo and Carmarthen—and that was in the pipeline).

When the provisional directors first met in London on 12 January 1859 Whalley was elected chairman. As money was short Davies and Savin said they would provide the Parliamentary deposit of £33,600 and the directors agreed—on condition that they were not held responsible personally for its repayment. Shareholders were to be guaranteed dividends of 1½ per cent through a 50 per cent rebate from the L & N for through traffic.

The directors decided that as the line would be passing through what they described as one of the richest mineral districts in Britain, they would seek powers to exploit any minerals found during construction. The provisional board met for the last time on 18 February as its Bill was being presented to Parliament.

Meanwhile the Central Wales Railway, strongly backed by the LNWR, had also completed its plans for a line from Knighton to Llandovery and had applied to the same session for its Bill. Both routes were parallel from Builth to Llandovery. The rival schemes went before a Commons committee on 16 March, but neither company got what it wanted. The Central Wales plan was agreed only as far as Llandrindod while the line from Llanidloes was cut short at Newbridge-on-Wye.

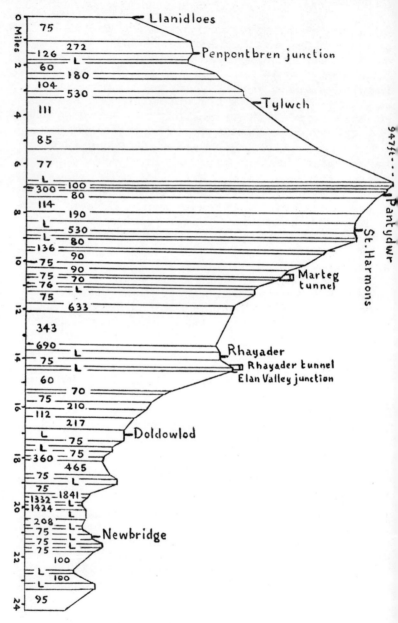

Gradient profile: Mid Wales Railway

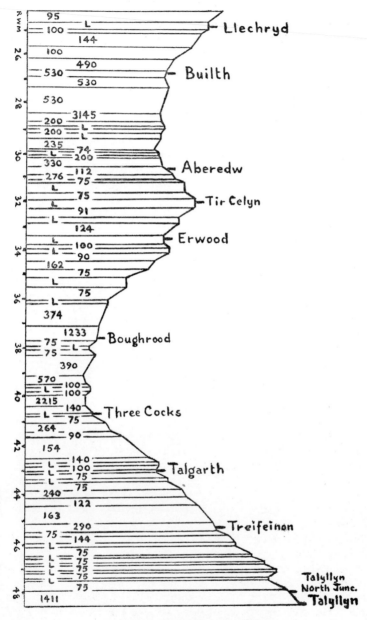

Gradient profile: Mid Wales Railway

The Llanidloes promoters were furious at their cut-down route and contended that, while they did not oppose the Central Wales plans, its promoters did everything possible to ensure the rejection of the Llanidloes line, especially through petitions from the Knighton Company and landowners acting in its interest. The Llanidloes promoters believed that it had been restricted to New-bridge because of an allegation by the Central Wales that it had not raised any capital to build a line to Llandovery. To counter this, they at once prepared a list of subscribers before putting the Bill to the Lords. The subscribers were bound to pay money only if the Bill was passed. There were hopes that the Oswestry & Newtown would provide £100,000 and the L & N half that sum and that the balance would come from the Shrewsbury & Welshpool. While the O & N agreed to its share the S & W hesitated and then did nothing—which might have been expected since the Bill was against the interests of the LNWR.

Litigation was costly: £3,559 13s 9d had been spent up to 31 March 1859. To get the company on its feet, Davies and Savin subscribed £60,000 and promised that their acquaintances would take shares worth £25,000. People living near Rhayader agreed to buy shares worth £10,000, while industrial backers included the rail-making Ebbw Vale Company (£15,000) and Sharp Stewart & Company, the Manchester locomotive builders (£5,000).

THROWN OFF COURSE

As a result of the cutback, the more local title of the Mid Wales Railway was chosen and this was consolidated in the Act to Newbridge, dated 1 August 1859. The first meeting of the Mid Wales board was held ten days later and J. E. C. Koch was appointed chairman in preference to Whalley as leader of the provisional board. R. S. France became secretary; Benjamin Piercy, engineer. The authorised capital was £150,000 plus £56,000 in loans, includ-ing an option for the L & N to take up £25,000—half the figure hoped for.

Whalley did not take his displacement lying down and bided his time before causing trouble. The rift between himself and the promoters began when Davies and Savin got an important stake in the company through their financial contribution. Whalley resented the contractors having such an influence and he was also at odds with them over the route, wanting to take the line well clear of Rhayader, where money was being so successfully raised. Savin used his influence to keep Whalley off the board when it was formed. It was the first of two major clashes he was to have with Savin —and lose. It came into the open at the cutting of the first sod of the Mid Wales, near Rhayader, on 2 September 1859. There had been two days of junketting already that week on the opening day of the L & N and the day after. Now, on the third day, Whalley presided at the Mid Wales ceremony. He was described not as chairman of the company, but 'chairman of the day'.

Things went wrong from the start. Everybody was fed up with the weather. As the *Shrewsbury Journal* commented: 'A viler day for rain and other discomforts than Friday was could scarcely be, even in Wales, which is a bold assertion.

'Amid the pelting of the pitiless storm,' it recorded, 'a procession headed by a brass band formed at Rhayader Town Hall and marched to a field close to the town. Whalley introduced the person who was to cut the sod—Mrs Pyne of Doldowlod Hall—saying that Mrs Pyne was of all persons in this part of the country, in the kingdom, or in the world itself, the person most entitled to perform the ceremony, for she was a descendant of James Watt, to whom the world was indebted for the introduction of the steam engine.'

The ceremony passed off without incident and 300 guests went into the luncheon tent where Whalley introduced himself as a defeated candidate for the direction of the Mid Wales Railway. He felt no humiliation, but satisfaction that this district, which he might call *his* district, had rejected him for a better man. He felt glad that they could say with the ancient spartan,

'Sparta hath many worthier sons than he'.

Then he went on to expand his bitterness and Davies and Savin both felt compelled to speak in their own defence. The ladies left the luncheon tent and the *Hereford Times* reported that waiters took away bottles and glasses from the tables 'in anticipation of a row more destructive than a war of words'. But the battle was contained in words and Benjamin Piercy restored calm without anyone coming to blows.

A final irony now remained to be enacted—the bowing-out not only of Whalley from the Mid Wales Railway scene—but of Davies and Savin too. This came about because after the guests dispersed from Rhayader calm of another kind settled on the whole project when no work was started. That was still the position when Davies and Savin split up over a year later. It meant they took no part in building it. It seems they had been losing interest in the line even before then for shareholders were told on 31 August 1860—two months beforehand—that there was to be a new contractor, Alexander Thomas Gordon.

To return to 1859, the calm which settled on construction did not extend to company politics and scheming and, with the line only authorised to Newbridge, thoughts were turned again to probing a route into South Wales. The MWR promoters had regarded Llandovery as their target for so long that they seemed blind to Merthyr Tydfil being the more natural—and central—gateway to the valleys. Now, as they started seriously to think about it in that light it proved to be too late: the Brecon & Merthyr Tydfil Junction Railway had been incorporated on the same day as the MWR—1 August 1859—to build north to Talybont, thus blocking the natural approach route from mid-Wales.

So, less than a month after incorporation, the MWR turned again to Llandovery, seeking powers this time to close the gap, now reduced to twenty-three miles, from Newbridge. It was heartened by a Board of Trade report which stated: 'This will supply rail communication to a district which is entirely unprovided with it and will form an important link, as it affords direct communication between the Northern Industrial Districts and South Wales'.

At the same time, the Central Wales Railway renewed its drive on Llandovery and the MWR decided to include in its Bill powers for branches to the proposed Hereford, Hay & Brecon Railway at Glasbury (Three Cocks) and the Brecon & Merthyr's proposed extension to Brecon at Talyllyn. These were lines additional to its main line to Llandovery. Besides forging a north-south link, the MWR saw itself as a channel for the cheap and abundant supply of lime to the counties of Radnor and Brecon.

Both Llandovery Bills went before a Select Committee in March 1860 and after a six-day hearing the Central Wales Extension Railway got the vote for the Llandovery line. The MWR directors were furious because they felt that, while they had no desire to exclude the CWER from fair participation in traffic arising from their extension to Llandovery, it had laid out its lines so as to exclude the MWR from any such traffic.

To get financial (and moral) support, the MWR offered to open its board to six directors—two from each of its neighbours. But the price it asked for the privilege seems to have been calculated by a secret means test. Hence, the Oswestry & Newtown was asked for £10,000, the Shrewsbury & Welshpool £30,000, while the price named for the Llanidloes & Newtown was £50,000.

The CWER Act received the Royal Assent on 3 July 1860—the

same day as the MWR got its sop-powers to join the Hereford, Hay & Brecon at Three Cocks and at Talyllyn the Brecon & Merthyr, which had got powers for its Brecon extension from Talybont on 15 May. The route to Talyllyn had, of course, only been intended as a branch line.

THE BATTLE FOR BRECON

Now the MWR had to set about building a route which involved a stiff climb from the Severn valley at Llanidloes and through the Tylwch Gorge to a summit at Pantydwr, 947 ft above sea level. From there it dropped into the Wye valley at Marteg and the next thirty-two miles to Talgarth were relatively easy going, although they involved bridging the Wye five times. The line now climbed out of the Wye valley and dropped into that of the Usk from Talyllyn. To cross the watershed a tunnel was needed, but this fell in the B & M section and that company planned to widen the one originally built by the Hay Railway. The MWR route needed only two short tunnels—372 yd near Marteg and 271 yd at Rhayader. The ruling gradient was 1 in 60. At Three Cocks, the MWR planned a north to east spur to make its own triangular junction but the spur was never built and as a result the boundary with the Hereford line was 29 ch towards Hereford. At Talyllyn, boundaries with the B & M were halfway along the north to west and the north to east curves, the triangular junction here being built as intended. In its Act of 3 July 1860 the MWR also got powers for a small deviation from the original route at Rhayader so as to avoid the 24 ch curve originally thought necessary for the line to Llandovery.

The Select Committee gave the MWR one concession in its Llandovery aspirations by insisting that the Central Wales must give it every facility for running trains to Llandovery. Subsequently, the CWR strongly resisted doing this and the MWR broke off talks, planning instead to take its case to the Lords. Even though Select Committees made stipulations, it was not easy to bring about co-operation between companies and promoters who were suspicious of every move made by a rival.

The fiercest tussle of all developed at the approaches to Brecon. Even before they were actually incorporated, the MWR and the B & M were suspicious of each other's intentions. But these suddenly melted in the face of competition from the Hereford, Hay & Brecon, which was incorporated only eight days later on 8 August 1859. The outcome of the battle was to give the Cambrian, with the passing years, the first of its two great limbs which stretched along the rugged coastline of Cardigan Bay and through the wooded country of the Wye Valley—two of Britain's great scenic routes.

The key to Brecon was held by a fourth company, which had been the first (on 7 May 1816) to reach the market town, strategically placed at road and canal junctions. This was the Hay Railway, authorised as early as 25 May 1811 as a 3 ft 6 in gauge horse tramroad. It ran twenty-four miles across the hills from the Abergavenny & Brecknock Canal at Brecon, through Talyllyn and Hay, to the Kington Railway at Eardisley in the Wye Valley. It held command of Brecon until the formation of the HH & B to build a route to the north of the tramway. Once the plans of the MWR and the B & M became clear, the HH & B decided to buy the tramway to keep them out. It is not clear whether at that time it intended to use the route of the tramway itself. To try and prevent the sale the MWR promoters bought Hay shares, but when shareholders met on 6 June 1859, the sale to the HH & B was approved by 239 votes to the 71 held by MWR interests.

The MWR and B & M now feared that the HH & B might try to keep them out of Brecon by asking an impossible price for the vital sections of the tramway—or might even refuse to sell. To protect their interests both companies went to Parliament and on 12 June 1861 the MWR was authorised to buy the Three Cocks-Talyllyn section of the Hay line. Powers for the B & M to buy the Talyllyn-Brecon section were given on 6 August.

The HH & B, on which work on the thirty-four miles from Brecon to Hereford had started on 10 April 1860, agreed to the MWR and the B & M having access to their portions of the tramway from 10 October 1861. At the same time it abandoned its section between Three Cocks and Brecon, receiving running powers instead. The original contractors, McCormick & Holmes, relinquished their contract and a new one was let to Savin & Ward. It was confined to work between Three Cocks and Hereford. As Savin & Ward were also busy constructing the B & M, relations with the Hereford company gradually drew closer and eventually resulted in amalgamation. In the break-up of the Hay, 23 acres between Pontithel and Talyllyn were sold to the MWR for £6,483 14s 2d on 19 August 1865—six days before the HH & B merged into the B & M. Because of the tramway's sharp curves only nine miles were regauged to standard, including three and three-quarter miles by the MWR and two and a half by the B & M. The latter included the Talyllyn Tunnel which had to be widened to the standard gauge.

OBSTRUCTION AND CONSTRUCTION

The moment the MWR felt it was time to start construction of its line, landowners who had often been sympathetic suddenly became obstructive by demanding high prices for land and the company was forced to use compulsory powers to acquire some of it.

The first section to be built was from the junction with the Llanidloes & Newtown to the new joint station at Llanidloes which, as it turned out, was first used by that company. By the beginning of 1862 the line was nearly ready as far as Penpontbren, but Alexander Gordon had done little other work. To get things moving Koch, the chairman, stated at the first board meeting in the new year—it was on 23 January 1862—that if the Llanidloes and Oswestry companies would subscribe to the work he would provide the rest of the money needed to ensure the completion of the line. Meanwhile, with work at a standstill, Piercy was ordered to creosote sleepers lying at Llanidloes.

A further move to strengthen the financial position was taken at the next board meeting on 21 February when fellow-directors unanimously agreed to Koch's idea of a personal credit squeeze. It meant that payments of £1,000 were to be withheld until the company had discharged its liabilities and work was nearing completion. A fresh contract was placed with John Watson (an associate of Savin) and James Overend on 26 March 1862. They were to get 223,000 ordinary shares; 117,000 debentures and 200,000 Lloyds bonds. They concentrated initial work on the hilliest section between Penpontbren and Rhayader, bridging the rivers Twlych, Marteg and Wye and making altogether seventeen river and eight road diversions. By February 1863 eight miles were ready for rails but completion was delayed by the need to brick-line the Marteg Tunnel, cut from solid rock.

The original plan to open the Llanidloes-Rhayader section in autumn 1863 was postponed because the rest of the route was nearing completion. Still there were troubles with landowners and the board said it regretted the activities of some who pressed to the utmost exhorbitant claims regardless of the benefit which the line would give them.

Intertwined, more on paper than anything else, with the MWR was the Manchester & Milford Railway. Little work had been done on the MWR when the M & M was authorised on 23 July 1860 to build some fifty miles from Llanidloes to Pencader to complete the grand route first conceived in the Railway Mania. The main stem was to run *via* Devil's Bridge. A branch was to run from here to Aberystwyth.

While the line to Pencader did not greatly interest the MWR the prospect of access to Aberystwyth was exciting. The two companies agreed a route and this was ratified by the MWR board on 6 July 1860. On 18 September, Piercy reported that he had made a trial survey from Rhayader to Aberystwyth in readiness for the deposit of plans in the next Parliamentary session. Although it was not until 1865 that the MWR applied to build a line from Rhayader to the M & M, that company got powers for its Devil's Bridge-Aberystwyth branch on 11 July 1861. It was an act with which the L & N was closely associated, getting powers to subscribe £20,000. But it only succeeded in raising half—and most of that went to help the MWR in its struggles.

Although anxious to make up for lost time, the only thing which the M & M did with any speed was to run into trouble. It was soon realised that the first one and a half miles from Llanidloes to Penpontbren duplicated the route for which the MWR had got powers the previous year. Various solutions were considered. At first joint ownership was considered with the M & M paying half the cost of a double line. Another idea was for the M & M to rent the section from the MWR, but this ended in a row and litigation. The final solution was amicable but complicated. A third railway, the L & N, was asked to build the section! To do so it had to get an Act —received on 17 July 1862—and this allowed it to build a joint station for the use of the three companies at Llanidloes and it was here that the general manager of the MWR had his office before moving to Brecon. As a complement to the M & M plans the MWR decided in October 1861 to build a branch from Marteg to Llangurig —and then dropped the idea within three months because of the money shortage. The scheme was revived in November 1862 at a time when the MWR was also seeking running powers over the B & M and the HH & B.

The Penpontbren section, finished by February 1864, was double, but only the down line was ever used. This agreed with the original intention, which was to double the line only when the L & N was doubled. From Penpontbren the M & M turned west for three miles to the village of Llangurig, sheltered under the Plynlimon range. This section was ready and signalled by February 1864 and earthworks were also completed for a short distance beyond the village. Apart from contractors' trains, only one goods train ever reached

LOCOMOTIVES—MISCELLANY

(24) 'Beaconsfield' No. 16—first 4—4—0, as built in 1878.
Note absence of brakes on locomotive

(25) Manning, Wardle 0—6—0, ordered as No. 60 'Aberystwyth' but
delivered instead as LBSC No. 219. Fitted with new chimney cap

(26) 'Queen' No. 15 as rebuilt by Aston with larger boiler in 1888
—the shape of things to come

ROLLING STOCK

(27) *Old four-wheel first and second class composite coach No. 34 on left with first class saloon built in 1889*

(28) *Old lime truck No. 356 in later years—still with dumb buffers*

Llangurig. Money had run out—not surprisingly since by 31 December 1863 only £7,953 had been raised by the M & M against its authorised capital of £666,000.

To conquer the mountains beyond Llangurig a spectacular line was planned with two tunnels totalling one and a half miles and a viaduct 280 ft high. Although a tunnel was started, work soon stopped.

The MWR's financial troubles were also never-ending. To meet the last spurt of effort the Oswestry & Newtown was asked in February 1864 to take up £70,000 in shares and the Llanidloes company £25,000.

The MWR was well beaten into Brecon by the B & M which had been there for over a year, its 19-mile single-line extension from Pant having opened on 1 May 1863. Construction had been started by Davies and Savin and after their split it was continued by Savin and Ward. They were then working the B & M in the same way as the Oswestry & Newtown and other lines to the north.

The HH & B was steadily completed from the west, being opened from Hereford to Eardisley on 30 June 1863 and extended to Hay on 11 July 1864, but trains could not, of course, reach Brecon until the MWR completed the Three Cocks-Talyllyn section. The whole of the MWR, including this gap, was ready for Board of Trade inspection in the same month, but the inspecting officer refused to pass some sections of track and a start was at once made on re-laying the whole of it with heavier chairs, although the unsatisfactory sections were tackled first. It was not until 23 August that a ceremonial trip was run from Llanidloes through to Brecon. Mineral trains began to run on 1 September 1864 and on 19 September a passenger service was started between Hereford and Brecon run by Savin and Ward (on behalf of the B & M) in succession to the GWR, with which the West Midland Railway was now merged and which had been working the shorter Hereford-Hay service. With the start of MWR passenger services two days later the east curve at Talyllyn was opened. MWR track re-laying continued slowly after the start of trains and only half the work was complete by May 1866.

Early station arrangements at Brecon were complex. The MWR and HH & B used the B & M's original terminus at Watton. Then the MWR had a row with the B & M and sought refuge for its trains with the Neath & Brecon at its station at Mount Street, opened 3 June 1867. Later, the MWR returned to Watton but moved from there and finally settled down in the new Free Street Joint Station, opened on 1 March 1871. Although it was owned by the B & M, the station was

H

built for the use of the four companies serving Brecon. It was built on the connecting line from Mount Street to the B & M at Heol Lladron Junction, east of Watton. At first the MWR felt the B & M's terms were onerous because of the limited accommodation it offered and because of the advantageous terms on which the B & M was letting the Midland Railway compete for the traffic it used to carry. The MWR was the last to sign a rental agreement with the B & M and it did not use Free Street until 1 May 1871. Only then did it consider the station important enough to house the general manager's office. The two older Brecon stations were now closed to passengers, although the B & M, MWR and Midland Railways continued to use Watton for goods and as a locomotive depot.

At Talyllyn the original MWR station at the north end of the triangle was closed in 1878 and trains started using the station which the B & M had opened on 1 October 1869. This was at the west junction. In 1895 the Cambrian made further improvements, adding an extension platform on the up (Llanidloes) side of the north curve, but beyond the junction. This was to allow its trains to clear the single-line entrance to the tunnel at the west end of the station. The three sides of the triangle were all multi-tracked, being used for the exchange of goods wagons between the three companies.

The MWR's main stations were built of stone and the junctions at Llanidloes, Llechryd, Three Cocks and Talyllyn, as well as Moat Lane, all later had refreshment rooms. There were no roofed platforms. The smaller stations had timber buildings and the original twelve had crossing loops. A single platform was added at Aberedw in 1869 (with local people paying £100 towards the cost), and ten years later at St Harmon's, where a siding for lime and other traffic had been opened in 1872. A local landowner built his own private halt at Tir Celyn, about one and a half miles south of Aberedw.

A scheme which would have given the MWR more traffic was that of the Worcester & Aberystwyth Junction Railway, incorporated 7 August 1874 to build a line via Rhayader and New Radnor. Parliament threw it out a year later, but in its wake came plans for a less ambitious link between Builth Wells and New Radnor. Plans were discussed at public meetings in 1876 but it was soon forgotten. Some twenty years later New Radnor became one of the targets for the East & West Wales Railway, designed to link the town with the MWR at Rhayader. This, too, was rejected by Parliament.

CHAPTER 8

The Weak Reality

As the line neared completion, the MWR desperately looked round again for any source which would provide through traffic. For a time things looked bleak—until neighbouring companies found themselves faced with the same problem. The first result of moves was an agreement with the Central Wales Extension Railway, which despite the early snubs it administered to the MWR in Parliament, was now anxious for through running and the interchange of traffic. A connection was agreed near Builth and the MWR got powers on 30 June 1864. It provided for a spur, 483 yd long, laid in the direction of its original target—Llandovery. It was stipulated that the connection was to be completed within three years under a penalty of £50 a day—unless the Board of Trade gave a certificate stating that the delay was beyond the MWR's control. A subsidiary clause allowed the MWR to acquire land for hotels.

In eager anticipation of the arrival of the Central Wales at the point of bisection the MWR opened a station called Llechryd (for Central Wales) in April 1866 and refinements added later included gas lighting and a water tank. The spur was brought into use seven months later: on 1 November 1866. This was the day on which the Central Wales Extension Railway opened the six and a half miles south from Llandrindod Wells to Builth Road. The rest of the CWER to Llandovery was not opened until 1 June 1868. The spur passed to the LNWR when it took over the CWER on 4 July 1870. An exchange siding was built the following year and in 1889 the MWR station was renamed Builth Road. 'Low Level' was not added until many years later.

While the spur was agreed but awaiting construction the MWR got powers on 29 June 1865 for a second and more ambitious connection with the Central Wales line. It was planned to run nine and a half miles from Rhayader to the CWR at Cross Gates between Llandrindod and Penybont. Because traffic was so light and money so short work was never started and the scheme was abandoned in 1876. The same fate befell connections which were planned with the Manchester & Milford under MWR powers of 5 July 1865. It was for a line from near Rhayader to Yspytty Ystwyth, three miles north of Strata Florida, and a branch to Llangurig. Powers also lapsed in 1876 and four years later the M & M abandoned, on 19 July 1880, its Devil's Bridge-Aberystwyth branch which put the resort beyond the direct reach of the MWR for ever. When the M & M abandoned its Llangurig-Strata Florida mountain crossing it gave the MWR the option of completion. The MWR made no move to exploit this 'generous gesture'.

Relations between the MWR and the B & M suffered setbacks at times and besides the rows at Brecon relations cooled off when the B & M sought powers in 1866 to double the section from Talyllyn to Three Cocks. The MWR felt that this would not only endanger its own traffic but that it was unnecessary as the single line had the capacity to carry four or five times more traffic in comfort.

The B & M's plan arose after a clash over fees for through traffic over this section and also forward from Talyllyn to Brecon. Both went to arbitration. But arguments like this did not help to solve the MWR's need for more through traffic and in December 1865 it set about trying to get other running powers over lines to the north and south of it. It also backed the moves by the Committee of Welsh Railways to bring about an amalgamation with the Cambrian, B & M and the Potteries, Shrewsbury & North Wales railways. After the Cambrian firmly and promptly refused to entertain the idea, matters rested until the MWR took fresh initiative on 11 December 1866 for a Welsh Union, seeing itself as 'the shortest link between South Wales and Lancashire'. The directors stipulated that the company's expenses in promoting a Bill should be restricted to £150 and the reason became clear only four days later when a fresh financial crisis loomed up. One of the influential shareholders—the London Financial Association Limited—of which Koch was secretary, warned the MWR not to issue Lloyds Bonds 'on any pretext whatsoever' without first consulting it. The board responded by asking Koch and other shareholders for their views on what it termed 'the present emergency'.

At the start of the year the MWR had warmly welcomed plans for a line from the Llandovery district and Llanelly to Brecon, Hereford and the Midlands since it anticipated that the traffic would flow via Talyllyn and Three Cocks. A Bill approved on 13 June enabled the MWR to subscribe to the Brecon & Llandovery Junction Railway.

After the Parliamentary battles of 1865 the MWR got running powers over the HH & B to Hereford and extended those over the proposed Merthyr branch of the B & M so as to link up with the Vale of Neath. With other companies the MWR was successful in defeating a Bill for the Vale of Neath to amalgamate with the GWR, which the two companies had agreed late in 1864. But the victory was hollow—a similar Bill went through Parliament in 1868.

Renewed pressure was brought to bear from the board in April 1867 for what was termed an 'urgent working agreement' with the Neath & Brecon. But the Vale of Neath-GWR amalgamation in 1868 brought fresh friction as the GWR refused to allow the MWR to exercise its right for through bookings to and from Swansea and other facilities *via* the N & B. The MWR went to arbitration and although the umpire, Captain Gallon, found in its favour, the GWR still refused full through bookings. In contrast, the MWR was more successful over the LNWR's take-over of the Central Wales line, on which it secured full through bookings.

The MWR pinned great hopes on the opening of the B & M's Merthyr branch on 1 August 1868 as it provided a direct outlet to Cardiff and the Rhondda and Taff valleys. From the opening day coal trains ran through to Birkenhead, where South Wales steam coal was in great demand for the ever-growing fleets of steamships.

Although the MWR always regarded the Hereford branch as a drain on its through traffic which would otherwise have gone north to Llanidloes, it threw away the one great chance it had to exploit it. It happened when it took over working it. To trace the events leading up to this we must go back to a series of apparently unconnected happenings in the Dulas valley in Glamorgan. They began with the opening of a purely local mineral railway from Neath to Onllwyn on 2 September 1864. Suddenly the local company developed greater ambitions which threatened to kill all the north-south traffic on the MWR. For on 13 July 1863 the Neath & Brecon Railway was authorised to take over and extend the mineral line to Brecon where it was planning to link up, not with the B & M, but the HH & B, and so introduce a through route from South Wales to Hereford.

For some time the B & M tried to keep the Neath & Brecon out of Brecon by promoting its own line to Devynock (and on through the mountains to join the Vale of Towy at Llandovery). This plan was backed by the MWR which was prepared to get powers to subscribe to the new line, but before this became necessary the N & B fell in with the wishes of the B & M by agreeing to join it, rather than the

HH & B, at Brecon. As a result, the B & M dropped its counter-thrust In any event, the N & B-HH & B hook-up would have faced serious trouble from the MWR which, with its command of the Talyllyn-Three Cocks section, would have been strongly placed to oppose any plans for a Neath-Hereford through route.

A stronger and more dangerous threat to the MWR came from the same quarter when the Neath & Brecon got powers for a 15-mile branch from Devynock northwards to the Central Wales Extension Railway at Llangammarch Wells, near Builth, on 29 July 1864. Construction started the following year and the first five miles of earthworks and bridges were finished before the contractor, John Dickson, went bankrupt. Work was then stopped and although it was never resumed the idea of completing the link was revived for a time around 1885 when the Devynock-Llandovery scheme was being reconsidered. The Llangammarch line would, with the Builth spur, have provided a direct route from Neath to the MWR and the Cambrian. But traffic would more likely have continued to flow north along the Central Wales to Shrewsbury and in any case the MWR would have lost revenue on the Talyllyn-Builth section if traffic was diverted from the B & M. Broadly, the bankruptcy of Dickson was one bankruptcy which seems to have helped the MWR and later the Cambrian.

A CHANCE THROWN AWAY

A return now from conjecture to reality and the time when the amalgamation that never was took place between the HH & B and the B & M, on 23 August 1865. It made no difference to the working agreement with Savin since he was already working the B & M. After Savin's failure six months later the B & M took over the trains to Hereford. But when the amalgamation was declared void by the Court of Chancery on 13 July 1868, the B & M threatened to withdraw its stock.

The MWR complained that while the B & M had improved its own Hereford services, it still had to run its own trains to Hereford. This position was resolved when the B & M withdrew and the HH & B asked the MWR to work its line for some years. As it was unsure of the traffic potential and was struggling so hard itself, it agreed to do so for only one year, starting from 1 October 1868. Relations between the companies were quickly strained when the HH & B asked for running powers over the whole of the Mid Wales line. The company regarded this as against the spirit of their friendly alliance secured by the working arrangement which it made on what it felt were liberal terms.

But despite opposition the HH & B got its powers, although it was refused agreements with the three big companies at Hereford.

Once the agreement with the MWR ended, on 30 September 1869, the Midland Railway got exclusive rights over the HH & B under an agreement which continued until it absorbed the company in 1886. One of the first things the Midland did on making the agreement was to claim the right to exercise the HH & B's running powers over the MWR. The reply was that the MWR did not mind the Midland working between Three Cocks and Talyllyn, although it did not consider this to be a legal right.

The Hereford line now became a traffic drain which the MWR could do nothing to plug and the position deteriorated because the Midland was interested, not in Brecon, but in the much more valuable prize of a through route to South Wales. A connection from the N & B at Colbren to the Swansea Vale Railway had been authorised on 29 July 1864. This lay in abeyance until Midland pressure brought the line to completion on 10 November 1873, when N & B trains started running through to Swansea (St Thomas'). The Midland got what it wanted on 1 July 1874 when its own trains took over all through workings from Hereford to Swansea.

A fresh outlet to stimulate traffic was mooted in June 1874 when MWR shareholders supported a Bill for an independent line from the Kington & Eardisley Railway at New Radnor to Rhayader, the agreement being that the MWR should work the line. Although it never got beyond the planning stage, the line would have been to some extent a popular tourist route since Kington was then the starting point for a daily coach and horse service to Aberystwyth, which was introduced when the Kington line was opened from Leominster in 1857. Kington was also, by mid-Wales standards, an important town having a population three times as big as that of Rhayader.

A more encouraging development came in 1883 when through workings to the coast of Cardigan Bay were agreed with the Cambrian and B & M. It was so successful that by the following summer there were through train services from Hereford, Swansea, Newport and Merthyr to Aberystwyth. By this time, hopes of trains reaching the resort over the M & M's branch *via* Llangurig had faded for ever. Whalley figured in the last attempt to save it when he wrote to the Cambrian on 8 September 1877 asking if the company would be prepared to offer working terms. It said it would consider advantageous ones if the line were restored from its derelict condition. It never was and in 1882 the track was lifted. Even though there was now no chance of the M & M going through the mountains it was still being charged by the MWR for joint facilities between Llanidloes and Penpontbren, where a branch siding survived at the Junction until after Grouping, and a square wooden M & M signalbox for even longer. The site of the line to Llangurig was sold about 1923, but the earthworks can still be traced for most of the way.

Ironically, the road from Llanidloes to Llangurig was selected in 1967 by the GPO for its first experiment in passenger transport, using a bus adapted to carry both passengers and mail.

Powers which the MWR got in February 1884 for working two other lines were never exercised. The Usk & Towy Railway (the company incorporated to link the Neath & Brecon at Devynock with the Central Wales Railway at Llandovery over the B & M's once proposed route) was never built. The other line—the Golden Valley Railway—was only half complete at the time the agreement was made and did not reach Hay for another five years, until 27 May 1889, although the first section from Pontrilas to Dorstone was opened on 1 September 1881. The working arrangement might have had greater attraction for the MWR if the projected line from Pontrilas to Monmouth had been opened. Savin had just started construction on it when he failed. The MWR saw the Golden Valley and Pontrilas-Monmouth lines as an artery for developing traffic from Gloucester to both North Wales and the Cambrian coast.

ON ITS OWN FEET

With the population of mid-Wales so tiny—there were probably under 20,000 people living in the area served by the entire line—one is tempted to consider whether it would have been built at all had it not been for the rat race among railway promoters to carve up the area in the vain hope that their line would become part of a great trunk route. The largest town served by the MWR was Brecon with a population of 5,000, but here the line was only one of several companies competing for its rather meagre trade. Llanidloes was, of course, an important centre, but its trade was more with Newtown, Oswestry and Shrewsbury, than with Brecon. Builth, at the time the line was opened, was a town of 1,200 people; Rhayader 1,000; while that grandly-named junction of Three Cocks served—and was named after—the local pub! Favoured by fishermen to whom the Wye was—as now—one of the most beautiful salmon rivers in Britain, the inn was described in guide books of the day as 'clean and comfortable'.

In competing for passengers from the tiny towns the MWR was up against the horse and coach and the horse omnibus services which, although slow, did flow along more natural routes of communication. The railways, in contrast, flowed across them. For instance, Brecon had daily coach services, not to Llanidloes, but south to Newport and Merthyr, west to Llandovery, east to Abergavenny and more locally to Hay. When these coach services were replaced by the railway most of the traffic went to the other companies which had better geographical lines of approach to Brecon. Builth had only coach services every other day to Hereford and Aberystwyth. Rhayader had a similar service to Llandrindod and Llandovery.

In view of its limited potential, it was hardly surprising that the Mid Wales even had difficulty in finding a company to work it. The first proposal was put in 1860 to the West Midland Railway as it was then working the HH & B. (The West Midland was formed on 1 July 1860 by the amalgamation of three straggling companies: the Newport, Abergavenny & Hereford, then working the HH & B; the Oxford, Worcester & Wolverhampton, and the Worcester & Hereford.) Although agreement was reached between the West Midland and the MWR, it was not carried out because of a dispute over payments proposed for through traffic.

The MWR let the question lie until, on 7 February 1863, it approached Savin as lessee of the O & N. Again there was no agreement reached. The next pressure came, not from the MWR, but from the Oswestry & Newtown in January 1864. It felt it was expedient that either it worked the MWR—or the MWR worked it. That exchange of views led to nothing more than running powers. While it was common for companies to exchange these with neighbours, they were not always granted—as the MWR found out when it approached the Cambrian soon after its formation. Finally, the task of working the MWR fell to the contractors and on 2 August it was reported to the board that Watson and Overend had agreed to do so as managers.

So on 21 September they began the service of three passenger and two mixed trains each way between Llanidloes and Brecon, including a through coach to Whitchurch and Crewe. There was also a return local working from Builth to Talyllyn. This timetable quickly became an embarrassment, not because it was too sparse, but because trains were too frequent. Trade was generally depressed throughout the country and this meant that traders had little reason to travel; and country folk had no money to spare. Yet the board decided not to reduce train frequency because it feared this would drive away what little traffic it had managed to develop.

Figures for the first half of 1865 brought little comfort to the directors. They showed that passenger trains had run 49,455 miles; goods, 32,760. Working expenses of £6,550 represented nearly 58 per cent of the receipts of £11,312. It was against this background that the MWR compared its costs in relation to other railways in the United Kingdom. It found that their costs averaged 46 per cent of receipts—a much healthier ratio. The MWR train density, although extravagant for the area, was well below average: the number of trains run for each mile of rail each year averaged, nationally, 10,095. The MWR figure was 3,425. But MWR expenditure per train-mile was lower—1s 7d against 2s 5¾d nationally. Working expenses each year for each mile of line were £272 on the MWR; £1,217 on other lines.

In that first half of 1865 the MWR got a welcome new source of revenue—the carriage of mails from 1 May. It meant that the post was now an hour later leaving Brecon and other places.

In the last half of the year 93,018 passengers were carried—85 per cent in third class, 10 per cent in second, the balance in first. Gross passenger receipts were £5,703. One encouraging feature during the summer was that nearly 5,000 passengers used the MWR to get to the coast. The directors forecast optimistically that there would be a material increase in traffic as the public got to know the beauty of its own line; the scenery of the Aberystwyth & Welsh Coast and the health and recreation which could be enjoyed on the coast. The mineral waters of Builth, Llanwrtyd and Llandrindod were valued highly by people who knew them, but there was a need of hotel accommodation at the spas.

Emphasis was laid more on passenger than goods services as there were few freight originating points. Goods carried in the last half of 1865 amounted to some 12,000 tons which yielded about a fourth of the gross receipts. The MWR lamented that the development of through goods services, which it so desperately needed, was hampered by lack of through booking facilities with the big companies. What mineral traffic did come helped little. For half of the 36,000 tons of mineral traffic carried in that period was iron ore from Northampton to South Wales routed forward over the B & M. It was only carried between Three Cocks and Talyllyn on MWR metals and allowed to pass at what was called 'a low rate'.

A further blow came with a summer cattle plague which halted the movement of animals.

The MWR found it difficult—if not impossible—to match the GWR's favourable charges for carrying coal from South Wales to Birkenhead and even when it did manage to quote for some of the traffic, its diversion was contested and taken to arbitration. Hopes of coal traffic increased when Ynyslas was mooted as a possible outlet for the export by sea of South Wales coal. Another possibility explored at the same time was the development of iron traffic from north (and possibly central) Wales to Dowlais and Merthyr.

The only traffic which did grow was that of lime—as envisaged by the promoters in the early days—and, in 1865, 8,000 tons were carried. Plans were also prepared for a delivery service from Savin's Talybont lime quarry to places along the line.

Crisis came when Watson & Overend gave up their lease and stopped working the line as a result of the failure of Savin, who had backed Watson financially. This left the company to do the job itself. In those troubled first two weeks of February the directors tried to interest other lines in working it, including the Midland and the Manchester, Sheffield & Lincolnshire—both companies showing an interest in Welsh railways at that time. But both turned down the MWR. When the MWR directors met shareholders on 27 February they reported that the upheaval had interrupted progress. Under the agreement with Watson & Overend they were to have worked the line and paid all outgoings for a rent. That due the previous month was not paid because of Savin's failure.

Passenger receipts continued to fall. A reduction of £1,300 in the first half of 1866 was put down to a drop in the number of agricultural travellers. Still the MWR maintained its original service, accepting courageously that expenses were comparing unfavourably with receipts. The risk was justified to some extent when the summer brought a rise to 7,000 in the number of passengers bound for the coast. The slackness of services, combined with the failures of Savin and Watson, meant a lot of rolling-stock was lying idle. To try and get some money from it, the MWR began loaning stock to other companies. Three locomotives and 50 wagons were out on hire in the early summer of 1866. All went to the Manchester, Sheffield & Lincolnshire and on 14 July the lot was sold to that company for £7,500, the locomotives being valued at £5,000. The bill, paid in December 1866 and January 1867, was promptly used by the MWR to meet claims for land which were still outstanding.

Another locomotive was sold to the Denbigh, Ruthin & Corwen Railway and the following year the MWR disposed of 17 carriages and 63 goods wagons.

To save locomotive mileage, an experiment was made in 1867-8 of B & M engines taking over the Mid Wales trains from Three Cocks to Brecon. It ended in a row, with the MWR claiming that the B & M was making extravagant demands. MWR locomotives then resumed running through to Brecon.

Early promise of creating a flow of coal traffic to Birkenhead, which came with the start of through trains from the day on which the Merthyr branch opened, quickly dwindled away. The MWR board was told on 23 January 1869 that its development had been checked by the need for good through services. Obviously, other companies were resisting the service and this was followed by another blow when coal for Birkenhead was diverted to coastal shipping. But a sudden and big increase in the number of steamships needing South Wales coal in the last quarter of the century brought about an increase in traffic and usually one coal train a day went north over the Mid Wales. A report of an accident to a Brecon & Merthyr train on 2 December 1878 shows that it included 22 wagons of coal for Birkenhead.

When the MWR relinquished working the HH & B on 1 October 1869, it got a new outlet on the same day with the start of a through passenger service *via* the Central Wales line at Builth. It was advertised as a much-improved route between South Wales and the north —but the claim was hardly supported by mileage since the new route cut by only three miles the distance between Brecon and Shrewsbury as compared with that through Hereford.

The following year the MWR complained that the Cambrian was depriving it of a through route by working the Moat Lane-Llanidloes section as a branch—an arrangement, it was stated, which annoyed the most seasoned travellers.

'NOTHING WILL DO MORE GOOD . . .'

Gradually—and only gradually—things got better and a 20,000 passenger increase in 1873 was hailed as a landmark as it meant the line had carried 2,000,000 in the first nine years. The same year the company felt flush enough to indulge in the luxury of buying two new engines and twenty-five new goods wagons—the first additions to stock since 1865. From then on, traffic picked up slowly until, in October 1879, the MWR felt it was sufficiently buoyant and stable to approach the Cambrian for a working agreement. An exploratory meeting which followed stressed that the Cambrian had always maintained that a united line would be mutually advantageous. The meeting led to the Cambrian inspecting the MWR line and books. That was as far as the Cambrian was prepared to go at that stage for when the directors considered a report on 20 March 1880 they decided to let it lie on the table. Fresh talks began three years later and were held in secret to avoid any outside interference and there were only guarded references to them in the board minutes. Secrecy prevented the Cambrian from giving any direct reply to a suggestion made by the Committee of Welsh Railways on 5 January 1885 that the company should have a joint traffic manager with the Mid Wales both on economy grounds and to help the development of a better link between North and South Wales. While the long negotiations continued, the MWR went on making its own agreements with neighbouring companies. Then in 1888, the agreement was announced. The reasons for the close secrecy became clear when the Cambrian's chairman, J. F. Buckley, gave the news to shareholders on 25 February and pointed out that it had been made under Acts which the company got twenty or twenty-five years earlier.

'If we had to get Acts now, we might have very much greater difficulty because the Great Companies have got all round North Wales and if we were to go to Parliament for Acts it is quite possible they might find it worth while putting us to great expense and trouble.'

A shareholder who suggested that the Cambrian should take over other small lines was also critical of the big companies. 'We are surrounded in Wales,' said W. Abbot of London, 'by powerful companies, the LNWR, the Midland and GWR. We know from experience how these powerful companies treat their weaker neighbours. If they see any sign of weakness they are down upon them like vultures, crushing the vitality out of them. But when they are developed by fusion, they frequently became valuable properties.'

The Cambrian took over the Mid Wales working on 2 April, but the agreement was dated 29 February (it being a leap year) and backdated to 1 January. Drawn up on the joint-purse principle, it was approved by the Railway Commissioners and it provided for the gross receipts of both companies to be shared. There were certain exceptions: the Cambrian was allowed to keep receipts from Aberdovey Pier and any money received from the Manchester & Milford for Llanidloes station. A sum of £730 a year rent for Llanidloes Joint Station was also excluded and £400 which the

MWR paid the B & M for the use of Talyllyn and Brecon stations. The maintenance of Aberdovey Pier was also outside the agreement. Of the rest of the gross receipts, the MWR was to receive 16 per cent up to £92,000 a year, 18 per cent above that amount.

The entry of the Mid Wales Railway into the Cambrian camp was clearly seen as the fruition of so much—and as the foundation of achieving so much more. As Benjamin Piercy commented:

'Nothing that has happened for a long time past will do more good to the Cambrian than this. The railways of Wales have been comparatively lifeless; it is now high time to put a soul into the system.'

The prophecy proved rather hollow if we believe the author of the *Tourists' Guide to the Wye*, G. Phillips Bevan, who wrote only four years later, warning travellers about

> the tender mercies of the Mid Wales Railway, which the tourist will find to be neither punctual nor swift.

He was particularly critical about Builth Road.

> This may lay claim to be about the most exasperating junction in the three kingdoms, not only for its general inaccessibility, but for the want of communication between the two stations, and the certainty of delay which rarely fails to meet the unfortunate traveller.

Not that there were many passengers to be delayed. Evidence to Parliament showed that in 1888 the Cambrian's gross weekly earnings per mile for passengers and goods were £19 6s 6d, while those of the MWR were only £12 4s 5d. There was nothing rich about the Mid Wales—except its scenery.

CHAPTER 9

Working the Line

EARLY TRAIN SERVICES

If it were true that the railways of mid-Wales were constructed in the short and hasty time of eleven years, so is it true that the time it took to build up a train service over them was long and slow. There was nobody and nothing to provide traffic of any kind in any volume.

The first passenger trains whose steam animated the Severn Valley between Llanidloes and Newtown on that early September morning in 1859 provided a service of three passenger trains each way. This was increased to four by the following year after the arrival of more coaches. The time taken for the 12-mile journey was 35 min. All trains stopped at all stations and none ran on Sundays. With the opening of the Abermule-Newtown section of the Oswestry & Newtown on 14 August 1860 all trains were extended to Abermule. The same day saw the completion of the Oswestry-Welshpool section and the provision of a more lavish service of six trains each way. All took 50 min for the 15½ miles, except one each way which omitted the Llynclys stop and took 2 min less. There was also the 'luxury' of two trains each way on Sundays. When the isolated portion from Welshpool to Abermule was opened on 10 June 1861, five of the six trains ran through to Llanidloes.

The next line to open—from Caersws Junction to Machynlleth on 3 January 1863—allowed four trains to run through to Oswestry from Machynlleth and four of the Llanidloes trains terminated instead at the Junction, now renamed Moat Lane, and made connections there. The Sunday service consisted of a train each way from Oswestry to Llanidloes and also to Machynlleth. As the line was extended, first to Borth on 1 July 1863 and then to Aberystwyth on 23 June 1864, the basic service remained unaltered except for the start of a through coach from Euston to Borth and then Aberystwyth—so much for the promoters' early hopes of attracting thousands to the coast. Complications were created by the opening of the Llanfyllin branch with extra trains between Llanymynech and Oswestry on 17 July 1863 and the completion of the main line to Whitchurch on 27 July 1864. As a result the whole timetable was recast.

Two up and three down trains were introduced between Whitchurch and Aberystwyth and also a train from Newtown to Aberystwyth and return to Oswestry. Shorter workings included two each way between Oswestry and Whitchurch and one each way between Oswestry and Welshpool. The Euston through carriages left at 9 a.m. and reached Aberystwyth at 5.55 p.m. The fastest time for the 95¾ miles from Whitchurch to Aberystwyth was 4h. 15m. and the slowest 5h. 25m. The best performance was by the 8 a.m. from Aberystwyth which ran the 18¼ miles from Oswestry to Whitchurch in 35 min, including a stop at Ellesmere. Most trains, however, spent from 10 to 20 min at the Oswestry or Welshpool stops, for engine changing.

A feature of the 1864 passenger working was that trains crossed four times a day on the short Welshpool-Buttington Junction double-track section. Four crossings were also made at Oswestry, two at Moat Lane and one each at Machynlleth, Newtown, Llanymynech and Montgomery. Traffic was so light in places that even a newly-opened station like Arddleen did not have even a daily service. All it got was two down trains on Wednesdays and Saturdays and one each on Mondays and on Welshpool fair days. Arddleen's up service consisted of three on Wednesdays, two on Saturdays and one on Mondays.

Sunday trains consisted of a morning one from Oswestry to Aberystwyth and an evening return. Connections to and from Llanidloes were provided at Moat Lane with both trains and there was also a return trip from Llanidloes to Oswestry.

Goods trains were the first to go into service on the Mid Wales Railway, running from 1 September 1864. During the interval before the start of passenger trains three weeks later, the Hereford service began using part of the route. On 21 September—two days after the HH & B service—five weekday trains began running each way between Llanidloes and Brecon, including a through coach to Whitchurch and Crewe. There was also a return local working from Builth to Talyllyn.

Of the Cambrian branches, the Llanidloes branch had two through trains to Whitchurch and one each returning from Whitchurch and Oswestry. Otherwise there were three trains each way giving main-line connections at Moat Lane. Llanfyllin had an initial service of

THE MID WALES LINE—1

(29) *Builth Road station (formerly Llechryd) looking north in 1936, with* GWR *0—4—2T No. 4874.* LNWR *line over bridge*

(30) *Elan Valley Railway Junction, a mile south of Rhayader, with rebuilt 2—4—0T No. 57 'Maglona', about 1898*

(31) *Brecon (Free Street) in 1903. Cambrian train in bay with Aston 4—4—0 No. 63; Midland trains on left*

THE MID WALES LINE—2

(32) *Rhayader station in 1904. Cambrian style box;* MWR *stone buildings*

(33) *Talyllyn old station closed in 1878. Typical* MWR *timber buildings*

five trains each way taking 30 min for the nine miles. This was cut to four within the year and the journey time increased to 35 min when Brongwyn and Llanfechain were added as stops in 1866. The Kerry branch also had four trains, taking a leisurely 25 min for the 3¾ miles. Also open was the detached line from Aberdovey Harbour to Llwyngwril with three trains each way taking 30 min for the 10¼ miles. There was also a short return working from Aberdovey to Towyn and three return sailings by the steam ferry to Ynyslas on the main line. The time allowed for connections varied between 33 and 45 min. The same service continued when the line was extended to Penmaenpool on 3 July 1865. With the completion of the coast line from Glandovey Junction to Pwllheli on 10 October 1867, the basic service was four trains each way daily with the best time of 6h. 45m. for the 152 miles from Pwllheli to Whitchurch. There were also some short workings on the coast. No Sunday trains ran on either the coast or the Llanfyllin or Kerry branches.

The carrying of mails was one of the revenue backbones of the passenger services and on 17 December 1864 arrangements were agreed by the Cambrian with the LNWR and the Aberystwyth & Welsh Coast Railway for the Government to pay Savin (as lessee of the line) for carrying mail. After he failed in 1866, fresh arrangements had to be made. One drawn up with the Post Office on 15 April 1868 provided for mail to be carried over the 69 miles from Aberystwyth to Welshpool at £39 a mile—a total of £2,691. The rate over the 49 miles covering Carnarvon, Pwllheli, Portmadoc and Barmouth was £12 (total £588) and there was a similar rate for the 26 miles embracing Glandovey, Aberdovey, Towyn and Penmaenpool (for Dolgelley). The total bill was £3,591.

In 1867, the Euston through coach service was extended to include a coach from Manchester (London Road) to Aberystwyth and Pwllheli, but the venture was short-lived.

Because of the haste with which the coast line was opened through to Pwllheli, Elias, the traffic manager, was able to issue his instructions only two days before and they were sent out from his office at Oswestry the moment the directors made the decision. Despite the haste, one rule was introduced as a result of experience gained on other lines. It laid down that passengers must arrive at stations five minutes before departure to make sure they had time to book tickets. More curious was the setting of station clocks at Greenwich Time, which was eleven minutes ahead of local time.

Timetables received only limited attention up to this time, but on

J

Summary of Trains between Welshpool and Buttington. UP.	1 L&NW Pass. A.M.	2 CAM. Pass. A.M.	3 CAM. Goods. A.M.	4 L&NW Goods. A.M.	5 CAM. Pass. A.M.	6 L&NW Pass. A.M.	7 CAM. Goods P.M.	8 CAM. Pass. P.M.	9 L&NW Pass. P.M.	10 L&NW Goods. P.M.	11 CAM. Goods. Wed. only. P.M.	12 CAM. Goods P.M.	13 CAM. Pass. P.M.	14 L&NW Pass. P.M.	15 CAM. Goods. P.M.	16 CAM. Mail. P.M.	17 L&NW Goods when requird P.M.	18 CAM. Goods. P.M.	19 L&NW Goods P.M.	SUNDAY. L&NW. Passenger. A.M.	SUNDAY. L&NW. Passenger. P.M.	SUNDAY. CAM. Pass. 1,2,3. P.M.
WELSHPOOL, dep.	6 35	7 10	7 30	7 35	11 13	11 25	12 50	3 30	3 55	4 10	4 45	6 5	6 55	8 55	7 50	9 0	9 45	10 30	11 45	9 30	8 55	9 0
Buttington .... arr.	6 42	..	...	7 40	...	...	1 0	...	...	4 20	4 55	...	...	9 0	8 0	...	9 50	...	11 55	9 34	9 0	...
" ....dep.	...	7 17	7 40	8 35	11 19	11 30	1 10	3 37	4 2	4 25	5 0	6 15	7 2	..	8 8	9 7	...	10 40	...	...	...	9 7

WEEK DAYS.

Miles.	UP.	1 Goods. A.M. arr.	1 Goods. A.M. dep.	2 Goods. A.M	3 Goods & Pass. 1, 2, 3. arr.	3 Goods & Pass. A.M. dep.	4 Goods. A.M. arr.	4 Goods. A.M. dep.	5 Pass. 1,2,3. A.M.	6 Pass. 1,2,3. A.M.	7 Goods. A.M. arr.	7 Goods. A.M. dep.	8
	*a*Aberystwith d.	.	6 0	..		..		.	..	8 0	..	8 30	.
4¼	*a*Bow Street.. „	6 20	6 25							8 12	8 50	8 55	
5¾	Llanfihangel „	d	d R						.	8 16	d	d	
8¼	*a*Borth .. „	6 50	6 55		.					8 22	9 20	9 50	.
10½	*a*Ynys-las..... „	7 10	7 25		.					8 27	10 5	10 10	
15¾	*a*Glandovey ... „	..	..	..	..	..			..	8 42		d	
16½	*a*Glandovey Junc. „	.	..	..	.	.			.	arr 8 44 dep 8 46		d	
17¾	Derwenlas Crossing	..	..	..	..	..	..	..	..	..	..		
20¼	*a*Machynlleth „	8 10	..	..	..	..	L	7 30	..	arr 8 56 dep 9 10	11 10	..	..
25½	*a*Cemmes Road.. „	..	..	..	..	..	7 47	7 52	.	9 22	..	..	.
30¾	*a*Llanbrynmair.. „	..	..	..	..	..	8 9	8 14	..	9 34	.	..	..
36¼	*a*Carno .... „	.	.	..	..	..	8 44	8 55	..	9 55	..	..	.
40½	Pontdolgoch . „	..	..	..	..	..	d	d	..	10 5	Goods & Pass.		..
42	Caersws ...... „	Goods & Pass.		..	..	..	9 25	9 35	..	10 12	1. 2. 3.		..
43¼	*a*Moat Lane Junc. arr.	1, 2, 3, arr.	dep.	..	..	..	9 40	..	..	10 15	a.m.		..
51	*a*Llanidloes.. dep.	..	4 50	..	..	5 10	..	..	..	9 50	..	11 30	..
48¼	Dolwen ...... „	..	..	..		..	.	..		9 55	.	11 36	
45½	Llandinam .... „	..	..	..	..	..	.	..		10 5	..	11 44	.
43¼	*a*Moat Lane Junc. arr.	5 10	..	..	5 30	..	..	..	..	10 10	11 52	..	..
	*a*Moat Lane Junc. dep.	..	5 40	..	..	..	..	9 55		10 18	..	..	..
46	Scafell Cutting. „	..	..	..	..	..	Tues.	d		d	..	..	..
47¾	*a*Newtown .. „	..	5 52	..	..	..	10 11	10 45		arr 10 29 dep 10 31	..	..	..
51¾	*a*Abermule .... „	..	d	..	..	..	11 1	11 11	Wednesdays only.	10 40	..	..	..
55¼	*a*Montgomery .. „	..	6 13	Pass.	..	..	11 25	11 42		10 49	..	..	..
57¼	Forden ...... „	..	d	1,2,3.	..	..	d	d		arr 10 54 dep 10 57	..	..	..
61½	*a*Welshpool { arr	6 30	..	A.M.	..	.	12 22	..		11 8	..	..	..
	{ dep	H	7 30	7 10	..	..	..	12 50		11 13	..	..	..
64¼	*a*Buttington .... „	..	7 40	7 17	..	..	1 0	1 10	☞	11 19	.	..	..
66¼	Pool Quay .... „	..	H	7 22	..	..	d	d	Pass.	11 24	..	..	..
67¾	Arddleen .... „	..	H	..	..	..	..	..	a.m.	Wed	..	..	..
69¾	Four Crosses .. „	..	H	7 31	..	..	1 28	1 38	1,2,3.	11 33	..	..	..
71¼	*a*Llanymynech .. „	8 5	8 35	arr. 7 36 dep. 7 38	..	..	1 44	2 0	10 40	arr 11 36 dep 11 37	..	..	..
72½	Pant .... „	8 40	8 45	d	..	.	2 5	2 10	10 45	..	Goods.		..
73¾	Llynclys...... „	8 50	9 0	arr. 7 44 dep. 7 46	.	..	2 15	2 25	10 50	arr 11 42 dep 11 44	P.M.		..
77¼	Oswestry .. arr.	9 15	..	7 57	..	..	2 50	..	11 0	11 55	arr.	dep	..
	*a*Oswestry .. dep.	6 0	..	8 5	..	..	..	..	..	12 0	N	3 30	..
79	Whittington „	6 5		8 9			.	.	..	12 4	d	d	..
82½	Frankton ... „	d		d				.	..	Tues	..	..	..
84½	*a*Ellesmere. „	6 25		8 23				.	.	12 19	3 55	4 0	..
87½	Welshampton. „	6 35		8 30					.	d	..	d	..
88¾	Bettisfield .. „	6 42		8 34					.	d	..	d	..
92½	Fenn's Bank .. „	6 53		8 42	..				.	d	..	d	..
95½	*a*Whitchurch arr.	7 3	..	8 50	..	..	..	..	..	12 45	4 45	..	..

H Passenger Coaches to be attached to this Train from Llanidloes to Welshpool only, except on Wednesdays, when they must be brought through to Oswestry. This Train will stop at Pool Quay, Arddleen, Four Crosses, and Pant on Wednesdays only. On Wednesdays this Train will leave Lanymynech at 8 20 a.m., Pant 8 25, Llynclys 8 30, arriving at Oswestry at 8 45 a.m.

L Passenger Coaches to be attached to this Train on Tuesdays only, from Machynlleth to Newtown.

N When this Train is late arriving at Ellesmere it must shunt there for the No. 9 Up Train to pass

R Stops when required by Signal, or upon intimation being given to the Guard, to pick up or put down 1st and 2nd Class Passengers only.

X Stops at Abermule by signal, to pick up Passengers for Stations beyond Welshpool.

Working timetable for June 1874

UP.	9	10		11		12	13		14	15	1	2
	WEEK DAYS.										SUNDAYS.	
	Pass. 1, 2, 3. P.M.	Goods & Pass. 1, 2, 3.		G. & P. 1, 2, 3.	Goods Pass.	Goods.	Goods. 1, 2, 3.		Mail. 1, 2, 3	Goods.	Pass. 1, 2, 3.	Pass. 1, 2, 3.
		P.M. arr.	P.M. dep.	P.M.	arr. dep.	P.M.	P.M. arr.	P.M. dep.	P.M	P.M.	A.M.	P.M.
ᵤAberystwith d.	12 30	..	..	4 15	..	..	..	..	6 0			6 0
ᵤBow Street.... ,,	12 42	..	..	4 33	..	..	..	..	6 12			6 12
Llanfihangel .. ,,	R	..	..	4 42	..	..	..	..	6 16	:		6 16
ᵤBorth .... ,,	12 51	..	..	4 52	..	..	..	..	6 22			6 22
aYnys-las ..:.... ,,	R	..	..	5 2	..	..	..	..	6 27			6 27
aGlandovey .... ,,	1 8	..	..	5 26	..	..	..	..	6 42			6 42
aGlandovey Junc. ,,	1 10	..	..	arr. 5 30 dep. 5 34	..	..	..	..				
Derwenlas Crossing	..	..	..	..	..	..	..	..				
aMachynlleth ,,	arr 4 25 dep 1 30	..	1 50	5 53	8 2 5	..	..	2 20	arr. 6 54 dep. 6 56	7 40		arr. 6 55 dep. 6 56
aCemmes Road.. ,,	1 42	..	..	..	2 20	..	2 35	2 45	7 12			7 12
aLlanbrynmair.. ,,	T	..	..	..	2 43	..	3 5	3 15	7 25			7 25
aCarno .... ,,	..	..	..	..	3 8	..	3 35	5 25	7 42			7 42
Pontdolgoch .. ,,	..	..	..	..	d	..	d	d				7 52
Caersws ...... ,,	d	3 0	3 5	..	d	..	5 47	5 50	7 57	..		7 57
aMoat Lane Junc. arr.	2 30	3 15	..	..	3 50	.:	5 57	..	8 1	8 55	.	8 1
aLlanidloes..dep.	2 0	3 35	..	..	..	..	..	..	7 35		7 25	7 20
Dolwen ...... ,,	2 5	3 40	..	..	..	..	..	..	7 40		7 31	7 26
Llandinam .... ,,	2 12	3 47	..	•	..	..	..	..	7 47		7 39	7 34
aMoat Lane Junc. arr.	2 20	3 55	..	..	..	..	..	..	7 55		7 50	7 42
aMoat Lane Junc. d p.	2 35	..	4 20	Pass. 1,2,3.	..	..	..	6 10	8 4	9 15		8 4
Scafell Cutting. . ,,	..	d	d	P.M.	..	..	d	d				
aNewtown .. ,,	2 46	4 35	4 50	6 0	..	..	6 25	6 35	8 15	arr. 8 29 dep. 8 35		8 15
aAbermule .... ,,	2 x 55	..	5 4	6 10			d	d	8 24			8 24
aMontgomery .. ,,	3 4	5 18	5 25	6 20	Mondays only.	Wednesdays only.	7 5	7 15	arr. 8 33 dep. 8 35			8 35
Forden ...... ,,	..	..	5 35	6 25			d	d				arr. 8 48 dep. 8 49
aWelshpool { arr.	3 20	5 53	..	6 35			7 35	..	8 50	10 20		8 50
{ dep	3 30	..	6 5	6 55		4 45	..	7 50	9 0	10 30		9 0
aButtington ... ,,	3 37	..	6 15	7 2		arr. 4 55 dep. 5 5	8 0	8 8	9 7	10 40		9 7
Pool Quay ... ,,	3 43	..	..	7 7		d	..	..	9 12			9 12
Arddleen ... ,,	..	..	..	P		..						
Four Crosses .. ,,	3 53	V	..	7 15		arr. 5 23 dep. 5 25	V	..	9 20			9 20
aLlanymynech . ,,	arr. 3 58 dep. 4 0	..	..	7 20		arr. 5 45 dep. 5 50	8 33	8 43	9 24	arr. 11 15 dep. 11 16		9 24
Pant .... ,,	d	d	d	d	..		..	..				
Llynclys..... ,,	arr. 4 10 dep. 4 12	6 45	6 50	7 28	..	arr. 6 0 dep. 6 4	8 52	9 0	arr. 9 30 dep. 9 32			arr. 9 30 dep. 9 32
Oswestry .. arr	4 24	7 5	..	7 40	..	6 20	9 15	..	9 42	11 25		9 42
aOswestry ..dep.	4 30	..	..	7 45	..	..	..	..		12 0		
Whittington .. ,,	4 35	..	..	7 49	..	..	..	..		d		
Frankton ... ,,	d	..	..	d	..	..	..	..				
aEllesmere.. ,,	arr. 4 49 dep. 4 51	..	..	8 3	..	..	..	..	arr. 12 30 dep. 12 35			
Welshampton.. ,,	4 58	.	..	8 10					d			
Bettisfield .... ,,	5 3	..	..	8 13					d			
Fenn's Bank .. ,,	arr. 5 14 dep. 5 16	..	..	8 23					d			
aWhitchurch arr.	5 26	..	..	8 32	..	..	..	..	..			1 30

P On Newtown, Welshpool, and Llanidloes Market Days this Train stops at Arddleen to put down Passengers, if required.

S This Train will only convey Passengers as far Moat Lane. where the Coaches must be attached to No. 10 Up Train.

T Stops when required at Llanbrynmair to pick up 1st or 2nd Class Passengers for Stations beyond Welshpool.

U Stops at Glandovey, Ynyslas, and Llanfihangel, upon intimation being given to the Guard, to put down Passengers booked from stations beyond Llanidloes and Welshpool.

V If these Trains are more than 10 minutes late arriving at Llanymynech they must shunt there for the Passenger Trains to pass.

• When Passenger Trains are not timed to stop at a Block Station, the Driver must not travel through the Station at a greater speed than FOUR miles an hour, so that he may with perfect safety deliver and receive the Train Ticket or Staff, and have the Train under perfect control in the event of any unforeseen obstruction arising.

Goods Trains must in all cases stop at the Stations at which they are timed to meet Passenger Trains, to exchange the Staff or Ticket.

Working timetable for June 1874

1 September 1868, in the face of criticism from shareholders and passengers, the board decided a more detailed approach was needed and the heads of departments were instructed to meet regularly to draw up monthly timetables. There were occasions when late running complaints were dealt with at board level. On 17 December 1867 the company's secretary was instructed to reply to a complaint about the 11.20 a.m. from Oswestry being delayed at Llanymynech. He stated that the day was exceptional, but the guard had been given instructions to prevent the same delay happening again. The following year the Cambrian protested to the LNWR after a slow-down of the 9 a.m. express from Euston, complaining that its schedule between Stafford and Welshpool was seriously damaging traffic to the coast. Not that the Cambrian service of 1874 was fast.

As can be seen from the working timetables on pages 130 and 131, the first up train took 5¼ hours to reach Whitchurch from Aberystwyth, while the middle-of-the-day mixed trains must have taxed many a traveller's patience. Taking 5¼ hours for the 57 miles from Machynlleth to Oswestry meant an average of 11 m.p.h. Yet this was better than stagecoach timings—although they could not have been far behind the slowest train of all: the 1.50 p.m. mixed ex-Machynlleth which, after galloping to Moat Lane Junction with one stop and covering the 23 miles in 1h. 25m., then waited 1h. 5m. before proceeding. It was due at Llanymynech at 6.30 p.m. (4h. 40m. for the 51 miles), but if it arrived more than 10 min late it had to wait for the 7.20 p.m. departure from Llanymynech to proceed before continuing to Oswestry.

It may have been this train which prompted a man to write to a local paper saying that he had been able to see his father safely on to the train at Welshpool—and then ride by horse to Oswestry in time to greet the old man on his arrival there! The Cambrian stated in reply, published in the next issue of the paper, that this mixed train *often* did not leave Welshpool until an hour after the adver-tised time and added that passenger coaches were only attached to these goods trains for the convenience of the public.

The three principal passenger trains all worked through from Whitchurch to Aberystwyth, but the mixed trains were all shorter workings, as were the seven daily goods over the main line at that period. They shuttled between the main centres and what through wagons there were had to be remarshalled for the journey forward.

Testimony to the sparseness of goods traffic on the Mid Wales Railway comes from the Llanidloes branch timetable. It had no separate goods trains at all; wagons arriving from the Mid Wales

Railway were sent forward by mixed train, of which there were four daily. The early morning mixed train worked through to Welshpool, where there was a good connection to Shrewsbury, but the others—and the three branch passenger trains—all terminated at Moat Lane.

The Llanfyllin branch had three passenger trains each way, two with through coaches to Oswestry, and also one mixed and one goods-only train. There was also a goods working as far as Llansaint-ffraid and return to Llanymynech. Yet there was no guarantee that passenger trains did not involve shunting as was shown in an accident report on the 4.40 p.m. from Llanymynech to Llanfyllin in 1881. This train, which carried through coaches off the 4.15 p.m. from Oswestry, also had a coal truck from Oswestry to Llanfyllin and also a lime truck attached at Pant. The rest of the train was made up of three coaches and a van drawn by the locomotive *Seaham*. Most of the eighty passengers had been to market at Oswestry but it does not seem to have been as well used as other trains for the train was axed in the next batch of economies. Thus in November 1877 the inland section lost not only the 4.15 p.m. from Oswestry to Welshpool and Llanfyllin, but also the 6.35 p.m. up from Welshpool and the early morning train each way to Llanfyllin. The coast lost two trains: the 1.45 p.m. from Machyn-lleth and the 10.35 p.m. from Pwllheli, but an extra train was put in at 8.30 p.m. from Pwllheli to Portmadoc.

At the start of a big holiday traffic drive in summer 1883 expresses were introduced to Lancashire and London, and Cambrian locomotives ran nearly 40,000 extra miles. The Lancashire service was a failure and the next year the express service to the coast was cut to one a day, which made good connections at Welshpool for London, Liverpool and Manchester. The double service of 1883 had cost £1,100 and the Cambrian felt this was too costly and it could afford only one daily express. But the summer timetable of 1885 advertised through coaches from Euston, Liverpool, Manchester, Swansea, Newport and Hereford to Aberystwyth, and also from Euston and Stafford to Barmouth. (See p. 179.)

The speeding-up of services which was made from time to time did not please everyone. Local residents complained that their local trains were often delayed to make way for expresses and they felt their trains should have preference as they provided revenue all the year round and not just in summer. Their complaints had strong grounds as the down stopping train which followed the Euston express was a mixed train and besides delay due to the express there were long waits at stations while shunting was carried out.

The best trains now ran from Oswestry to Aberystwyth in about 3½ hours, although the inclusive speed was only 22½ m.p.h. The 2.25 p.m. and 5.57 p.m. down trains now arrived at Aberystwyth at 5.57 p.m. and 9.25 p.m. The 'down mail', 4.40 a.m. from Welshpool, took 2¾ hours for the sixty-two miles to Aberystwyth. Up trains were all allowed longer, being given what has come to be known as 'recovery times'. This was because the Cambrian dared not incur the displeasure of the LNWR by arriving late at Welshpool or Whitchurch for fear of connections being withdrawn. Thus the fastest up train, the 12.50 p.m. from Aberystwyth, arrived at Oswestry at 4.48 p.m., but this was still 58 min quicker than the same train in 1874.

The delivery of a second pair of 'Beaconsfield' 4—4—0s in 1886 enabled a speed-up to be introduced on the main line and the fastest trains now covered the seventy-five miles between Machynlleth and Whitchurch in 2h. 21m. at an average speed of 28 m.p.h.—a comparatively respectable increase of 6 m.p.h. The best down train, the 1.40 p.m. from Whitchurch, took 3h. 41m. to reach Aberystwyth, but this time included no less than 29 min spent standing at four intermediate stops. The average speed, exclusive of stops, was 34½ m.p.h.

When the Cambrian took over working the Mid Wales Railway in April 1888 it introduced a through express in each direction between Moat Lane and Brecon. Taking 2h. 17m. for the sixty miles, the average speed worked out at 26 m.p.h. including stops, or 30½ m.p.h. exclusive.

There were still no expresses on the coast line, however, the 'fastest' trains taking 2¾ hours between Machynlleth and Pwllheli. Other trains took longer mainly because of waiting at Barmouth for a Dolgelley connection. The Dolgelley branch service at this time was quite good, consisting of seven passenger and two goods each way daily, the passenger trains taking 25 min between Dolgelley and Barmouth.

The Kerry branch service consisted of two passenger and two mixed trains each way daily with an extra passenger train in the summer and also on Monday, Tuesday and Saturday. All trains took 25 min each way.

Sunday services still consisted of only the solitary up and down mail between Oswestry and Aberystwyth and connections from Moat Lane to Llanidloes. No Sunday trains ran on other lines. With no connecting service, Glandovey Junction was closed on Sunday, as were Scafell, Arddleen and Pant stations.

A feature of the timetable at this period was the large number of conditional stops. Some stations only had trains calling by request. They included Arddleen, Bryngwyn, Frankton, Scafell and the intermediate stations on the Kerry branch. This policy was carried out in deference to Parliament's wishes that at least one train a day must stop at all stations—although it did not actually have to come to a stop if there was no traffic.

MANAGEMENT AND STAFF

As an employer, the Cambrian was held in mixed esteem. In the rural areas it was the biggest single employer and while its arrival provided greatly-needed jobs which kept some men from drifting away to the rapidly-growing industrial towns, it also allowed the company to pick and choose its staff. It had the whiphand in dictating conditions of work and, even though trains were infrequent, hours worked by the staff were long and arduous. They included spells of anything up to 36 hours of continuous duty. Pay was low and discipline strict. One of the earliest rules—issued on 12 October 1864—laid down that staff had to carry a copy of rules and regulations everywhere while on duty. If they were found without them they faced a fine of five shillings—quite a sum in those days.

For some years after its formation the Cambrian was run mainly by chief officers who had served the constituents with distinction. On amalgamation, George Lewis was the obvious choice for the top post of secretary and general manager, having been secretary to three of the four constituent companies. His appointment was ratified on 1 January 1865 at a salary of £700 a year. Although Benjamin Piercy was retained as consulting engineer, his assistant, George Owen, was appointed the Cambrian's engineer at £600 a year. He had been engineer to several of the constituent companies. The other important post, of company solicitor, went to Abraham Howell from the Oswestry & Newtown Railway, who received £1,000 a year, with extra if there was heavy Parliamentary pressure. Other posts were filled after Savin, who was working the line, went bankrupt on 5 February 1866. The following day Elijah Elias was appointed traffic manager to keep trains moving.

The position of traffic manager was the Cambrian's 'problem seat', rather like what a football manager's job has become in recent years—vulnerable to criticism from people above and below. Elias held it until 1 August 1870 when Henry Cattle was appointed. He did sufficiently well to be awarded a testimonial when he resigned on 30 November 1878. After he left, the job remained vacant through the succeeding years of trade and traffic depression until John Conacher, who had joined the company in 1865, became secretary in March 1882. He was put in to replace Lewis who was then offered the post of traffic manager. As the post of general manager was left vacant, Lewis was given the mandate of improving the train service but he was unable to get on with Conacher and resigned on 31 August. The next traffic manager, Edward Liller, was appointed from 1 November but he was unable to do any better under Conacher, who was a hard taskmaster, and he was given three months' notice and £100 for removal expenses on 30 September 1883. The board blamed him for a continued decline in revenue, but it was not a view which was universally held.

He found a champion in the indefatigable shareholder Bryan who at the next meeting claimed that Liller had been most conscientious in advertising the line and had got £100 from the 'watering places'. Liller, stated Bryan, had been badly treated by the company. But Liller still left and Conacher went on to manage the various departments on his own despite the extra burden of being appointed Receiver when the Cambrian went bankrupt a year later.

Other important positions in the seventies and eighties were those of goods manager (J. Shepherd), carriage and wagon works foreman (J. Richards) and chief inspector (George Thomas). Also during this era and until 1900 the company solicitor was H. C. Corfield, who had succeeded Ashurst and Morris, who in turn had replaced the pioneer Abraham Howell.

By the time the Cambrian was established, many of the staff of the constituents had faded from the scene. The distinction of being the first secretary of a railway in mid-Wales fell to John Jenkins who was secretary of the Llanidloes & Newtown for about a year from 1853. He was succeeded by Thomas Hayward who held office until 1861, when B. Tanner took over. One of the earliest traffic managers was R. B. Elwin, appointed to the Oswestry & Newtown in October 1860. The first traffic manager of the Mid Wales Railway, Frederick Broughton, left in August 1875 to become general manager of the Great Western of Canada Railway and he was succeeded by Frank Grundy.

The Cambrian's chain of management locally was through stationmasters and when they erred consequences were strong—as the man at Fenn's Bank, J. Baddiley, found out on 15 September

1865 when he was sacked for leaving his station without putting somebody else in charge.

Stationmaster's pay at the smaller stations was 15 shillings to 16 shillings a week and their uniform included the traditional silk hat. A well-known stationmaster in the sixties was John Ceiriog Hughes of Llanidloes, one of the most famous of Welsh bards. He moved to become manager of the Van Railway in 1872.

Stationmasters who did not send in accounts on time were reprimanded under instructions issued on 14 April 1871. These stated that the penalty for repeating the offence was dismissal.

From June 1886 it became compulsory for guards and shunters to use coupling sticks.

Specialised knowledge gave locomotive men a generally greater tenure of security. Because of Savin working the line at first, the Cambrian did not appoint its own locomotive superintendent until it had to—and then chose a man on the spot. He was Alexander Walker who had been looking after Savin's locomotives and he took office on 26 April 1866. He stayed with the Cambrian until he retired on 31 March 1879. He nearly left ten years earlier when he was given a testimonial on applying for a similar job with the London, Brighton & South Coast Railway. He did not get it and stayed on at Oswestry receiving, in 1871, a salary increase of £100 a year. When he retired his assistant, William Aston, was made foreman in charge, but under George Owen as engineer. Aston had joined the Cambrian in 1865 from the LNWR, having been trained under John Ramsbottom at Crewe. This early influence was apparent in the similarities in appearance between Aston's locomotives and those of the LNWR. Aston was officially appointed locomotive superintendent on 1 September 1882 for a trial period and his position was ratified from 1 June 1884. The Mid Wales Railway appointed G. F. Ellis as its locomotive superintendent in 1875 but when the Cambrian took over he had to take a more secondary post as foreman at Llanidloes.

While the Cambrian used the LNWR engine shed at its north-eastern extremity at Whitchurch, it had its main shed only a short distance away at Oswestry. The other Cambrian sheds were at Welshpool, Moat Lane, Machynlleth, Aberystwyth; Dolgelley (Penmaenpool), Portmadoc, Pwllheli on the coast; Llanfyllin, Kerry and Llanidloes on the branches. The Mid Wales Railway also had its own shed at Llanidloes and others at Builth and Brecon, where the small wooden building, destined eventually to collapse, was built alongside that of the Brecon & Merthyr at Watton yard. The

Midland also used the B & M's Brecon shed but the B & M kept a shed at Talyllyn for its own exclusive use.

The Cambrian's undisputed hub was Oswestry. Besides the head offices and largest shed, Oswestry was the site of the main locomotive, carriage and wagon works. These also came under the locomotive department. They were developed as a result of pressure which grew as the Montgomeryshire railways developed in the early sixties. The initiative came in 1863 from the Oswestry & Newtown, the most advanced of the companies. On 24 April it asked Benjamin Piercy to prepare plans on the lines of the Shrewsbury shops of the Shrewsbury & Hereford Railway. At the end of August the O & N agreed in principle to shops being built—at Oswestry—at a cost of £28,000.

Little had been done towards building them by the time the Cambrian was formed and by then the need for shops was so pressing that, at its first meeting, the Cambrian board asked Savin to prepare detailed specifications to the designs of the Manchester locomotive builders, Sharp, Stewart & Company. The board also replied to a plea from the people of Welshpool asking for the workshops to be built there instead of at Oswestry. It explained that it had already bought land at Oswestry and had spent a lot of money on planning. Welshpool had regarded its claim as strong because of its more central position on the main line and also because it had plenty of land adjoining it. Savin also maintained a small repair shop there.

In contrast to the land available at Welshpool, the Oswestry site required some excavation out of the side of a dominating hill called Shelf Bank. It was close to where the first sod had been cut of the Oswestry, Ellesmere & Whitchurch Railway, near the Whitchurch end of the station on the down side opposite the GWR station. While Savin built the works, the erection was supervised by George Owen, and Sharp, Stewart & Company designed and built the machinery under the supervision of the architect, John Robinson, also of Manchester.

The works were brought into partial use in January 1866, but when Savin failed the Cambrian was left with the job of completing them. This it did by August of that year and the small Welshpool shop was then closed.

The Oswestry locomotive, carriage and wagon shops were housed in one building, 812 ft long by 210 ft wide, covering an area of 170,520 sq ft. Some 4,145,952 bricks were used together with 28,483 ft of Baltic timber, 92,520 superficial ft of slating and 25,298 ft of

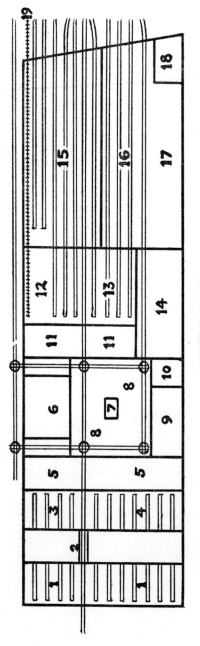

OSWESTRY WORKS

1 Locomotive erecting shop
2 Traverser
3 Tender shop
4 Boiler shop
5 Locomotive machine shop
6 Stores with offices over
7 Wash-houses and WCs
8 Open yard
9 Boiler house
10 Brass foundry
11 Smithy
12 Carriage machine shop
13 Carriage building shop
14 Foundry
15 Wagon shop
16 Paint shop
17 Grease shop
18 Sheet room
19 2 ft gauge tramway to
   timber drying

glass. Features were a tower surmounted by a weather cock—a fine representation of an 'Albion' class 2—4—0 passenger engine seen broadside; an octagonal chimney 150 ft high, and a main entrance from the town provided by a footbridge spanning nine Cambrian and four GWR roads.

The works were divided with the offices, stores and wash-houses in the centre. At the station end were the locomotive shops; at the Whitchurch end the carriage and wagon shops. The locomotive erecting shop had a central traverser serving twelve roads on each side, including the entrance and through road which was kept clear. The other roads could each accommodate a single locomotive or tender. They were moved by hand by 'pinching' as far as the enclosed yard outside the shop, where the works shunter took over. The scrap siding was in this yard.

At the other end of the works a network of sidings fanned out across an open yard and eleven, including the through road, continued into the carriage and wagon shops. While a lot of carriages and wagons were built in the workshops, only two locomotives were actually constructed at Oswestry, although many were extensively rebuilt.

The Mid Wales Railway had its locomotive headquarters and small carriage and wagon works at Builth, but most wagon repairs were carried out by Thomas' Wagon Works at Llanidloes. This practice ceased in 1874 and the MWR was forced to extend its Builth Wells shops in 1875-7 at a cost of £855. They continued in use after the Cambrian took over in 1888, but closed in 1903 when the equipment was transferred to Oswestry.

The Cambrian also had additional wagon repair shops at Aberdovey. These were opened on 19 October 1880 because of the isolation of Oswestry works from the coast and to avoid the time and cost of sending damaged wagons over Talerddig. The need was so pressing that over 100 wagons went through the Aberdovey works within a few weeks of opening.

A feature of Cambrian passenger stations was the low height of the platforms which required two footsteps to be provided on each side of all passenger coaches. Many of the original two-platform stations were without footbridges at first, but most had got them by 1900. The system was without island platforms except at three-platform stations: Afon Wen, Dovey Junction, Moat Lane, Llanidloes, Abermule, Welshpool, Llanymynech and also the stations at Whitchurch and Brecon used by the Cambrian. There were four platforms at Barmouth Junction and Three Cocks but at the latter

Cambrian trains used only two of them. The largest station, Aberystwyth, had five platforms.

Permanent way in the mid-eighties consisted of bull-headed rails, 24 ft long (and even slightly shorter on curves), weighing 82 lbs to the yard.

The earliest stations were lit by oil lamps. At first many used seal oil, but quickly changed to mineral oil. Gas lighting was introduced on the system through the more important early stations like Newtown, Machynlleth and Ellesmere, where it was fitted in the winter of 1867. It soon spread to all stations within reach of a public supply.

Several of the early stations were temporary affairs due to lack of money and passengers often complained about their poor facilities—or absence of them. One of the strongest protest groups grew up at Newtown and it was only silenced by an announcement on 26 October 1868 that the station was to be rebuilt at a cost of £1,200.

Some complaints were more trivial: in February 1871 a petition was handed to the management requesting a drinking fountain at Moat Lane.

But petitions were not needed about drinking facilities of another kind, as these were provided at most of the principal stations. Considering the sparseness of the passenger traffic, the system was well provided with refreshment rooms which must have helped to console travellers on slow trains waiting for even slower connections. By autumn 1872 rooms were open at Oswestry, Llanymynech, Welshpool, Machynlleth, Borth and Aberystwyth on the main line; at Barmouth Junction, Portmadoc and Afon Wen on the coast; Llanidloes, Builth, Llechryd and Three Cocks on the Mid Wales. Later one was provided at Pwllheli. It was perhaps to encourage passengers to use the refreshment rooms that several stations were built without roofs over the platforms—although the official reason given to local authorities which often pressed for them was shortage of money. In the refreshment rooms, first- and third-class passengers were segregated.

Often the rooms were run by local innkeepers who contracted to run them either singly or in groups. The arrangement was reasonably successful but the Cambrian soon saw them as a good revenue potential and in 1882 sought powers to run them itself. But it never did and from the late eighties a single firm, Spiers & Pond Ltd, had the lease for most of the rooms on the system.

ACCIDENTS AND PREVENTION

However enterprising the Cambrian and its constituents were in developing refreshment facilities in the early days, they were woefully slow in providing—or even attempting to provide—the most elementary of safety devices like continuous brakes. Not even the heavy gradients acted as a spur.

Among the earliest of safety ideas was that of an external communication cord introduced from about 1870. It ran through eyelets on the edge of carriage roofs to link up with the guard. In an emergency an unfortunate passenger had first to remember on which side of the coach the cord was fixed and then he had to open the window and grope upwards—perhaps in the dark. Yet once having found the cord his troubles were not over for he had to haul into his compartment several feet of it before he could attract the guard's attention.

For his part, the guard had only a handbrake to try and stop the train and he had to hope that as he applied it, the driver would realise what was wanted and help in bringing the train to a halt.

Initiative towards introducing continuous brakes came not from the Cambrian—or, indeed, other companies—but from the Board of Trade. Towards the end of the seventies it applied pressure to all railways which were not using them and the move resulted in the Railways Returns (Continuous Brakes) Act of 1878. This made such brakes compulsory on passenger trains.

But the wrangle was not at an end: in June 1880 the Board wrote asking the Cambrian to advise what progress it had made and whether it could state a date when the work would be finished. Even this failed to rouse the Cambrian to action, although it should be pointed out that continuous brakes were at that time still in the experimental stage and there was a lot of resistance to them. At a conference of twelve leading railways, including the LNWR and GWR, which was called in April 1881 to try and agree on a standard brake system, nine companies favoured the simple, non-automatic, vacuum brake. They all agreed, however, to adopt the Midland coupling for brake hoses as standard.

Despite the passing of the 1878 Act, a Railways (Continuous Brakes) Bill, which proposed compulsory *automatic* brakes for all passenger trains, was thrown out by Parliament in 1882-3 as there was still not enough confidence in the reliability of automatic brakes. Even so, when the Cambrian did finally decide in 1885 to adopt continuous brakes, it selected the fully-automatic vacuum type.

The first engines built with vacuum brakes were the two 'Beaconsfield' 4—4—0s delivered in 1886. Fourteen other passenger engines and sufficient carriage stock were also fitted from this year to enable main-line passenger trains to be automatically braked, but it was not until the mid-nineties that all passenger trains were fitted.

Another safety feature used by the Cambrian was single-line train staffs to prevent two trains using the same section of single line at once. After the installation of the telegraph on the main line to Aberystwyth in 1865 a more flexible arrangement, the staff and ticket system, was used. Stationmasters were empowered to issue written authority to drivers to proceed and retain the staff for a following train.

Tyer's electric tablet instruments were being installed by 1888 but it was 1890 before the main line was protected.

One thing to be said in favour of the early trains is that their slow speed prevented a number of minor mishaps from turning into major disasters. Not until 1897 was a passenger killed on a Cambrian train, although the first serious accident had occurred before amalgamation. It happened in November 1861 on the Oswestry & Newtown Railway near Abermule—the scene, many years later, of the last and worst accident on the line. The 1861 accident involved an up goods train from Newtown to Welshpool. After collecting three trucks from the sidings and taking water at Abermule, the engine crew and the guard decided that there was just time for a quick drink in the local hostelry. They stayed longer than they intended for when they came out they realised they were well behind schedule and the driver, known as 'Hellfire Jack', tried to make up lost time over a stretch of line only completed four months earlier and not then fit for fast running. The engine was derailed and overturned and both the driver and fireman were killed. At the subsequent inquiry it was held that the accident was due to 'furious driving' and there was no blame attached to the O & N.

There was one instance of the minor accidents in the early days when working rules and precautions were not as strict as they became in later days in 1869, when a driver unexpectedly found signals against him and being unable to brake in time, hit a special carrying the chairman. It happened on 25 November when a goods was descending the bank from Talerddig to Newtown. The driver, Burke, was accustomed to a clear run through to Moat Lane and when he found the signals at Carno against him was unable to stop on the greasy rails. He ran through the station and hit the special approaching from the opposite direction and taking the chairman, Earl Vane, home to Machynlleth. Little damage was done but Burke was sacked, together with the Carno stationmaster, Patterson, who was held partly to blame. An appeal for their reinstatement signed by people at Machynlleth was unsuccessful.

A collision between LNWR and Cambrian trains at Welshpool on 18 November 1870 resulted in the companies deciding to share the costs, while each paid for its own repairs—an early example of the 'knock-for-knock' agreement. There were novel ways of settling claims as well in those early days—in February 1868, Elias, the traffic manager, was reprimanded for issuing passes as part compensation for a minor accident. There were also rewards for quick thinking which prevented accidents. A man got £3 3s 0d in September 1868 for stopping a mixed train; another got £2 2s 0d for stopping a train from Machynlleth to Moat Lane.

Soon after the formation of the Cambrian, the station building at Arddleen was burnt down in January 1865. No one was hurt and although the cause of the fire was never found, it could have been caused by a spark from a passing train. The Cambrian found it was not insured against fire risk to station buildings and so immediate steps were taken to get them covered.

Two crashes which both resulted in the death of engine crews were unfortunate and it was found that no-one was to blame. The first, in February 1868, occurred at Caersws when the Severn was flooded after severe storms. The morning goods from Newtown to Machynlleth was involved. The driver had already crossed the river bridge earlier that morning and found it safe. He was on the return journey, still in darkness, when the floods washed away part of the embankment leading to the bridge and the gap under the track was not noticed. The driver and fireman both died as the engine fell down the bank. The early morning train from Aberystwyth to Whitchurch was only just stopped short of crossing a badly damaged bridge at Pontdolgoch immediately after the Caersws incident.

The second fatal accident, in 1883, was also due to bad weather —and a set of unusual circumstances. While it is well-known that a loud noise can start an avalanche of snow in mountains, it must be remarkable for the laboured exhaust of a steam locomotive to set off a landslide. Yet this happened *twice* on the precipitous section of the coast line between Llwyngwril and Barmouth Junction at Friog. The line is cut into the cliff face 86 ft above the rocky

THE MID WALES LINE—3

(34) *The junction that never was: Penpontbren. Looking north to Llanidloes with Manchester & Milford line curving in from left. Note: signalbox with slotted signal in drop position opposite*

(35) *Collapse at Brecon: the former* MWR *engine shed at Watton*

OSWESTRY WORKS

(36) *Locomotive erecting shop, October 1909. Traverser through arches on right, 2—4—0 No. 55 in foreground*

(37) *Wagon shop, 1904. 15-ton open wagons under construction*

shore of Cardigan Bay where the massive ramparts of Cader Idris reach down to the sea. When the line was first passed by a Board of Trade inspector in 1865, he imposed a speed limit of 4 m.p.h. and insisted on regular inspection. There were occasional falls of rock, but a close watch was kept and the Cambrian was quick to react to any threat of danger. When the Board wrote in December 1870 saying it had received a letter complaining about the dangerous state of the line in the cutting, the Cambrian was not too concerned in view of its regular inspections and simply asked the Board to send an inspector.

The first landslide was on the evening of New Year's Day 1883 as the 5.15 p.m. train from Machynlleth to Barmouth was approaching the cutting, after a day of severe storms. The coast road is also cut into the same cliff, but more than 100 ft above the railway, and when the line was built the road was also affected by the cutting away of the cliff and a dry stone wall was constructed by Savin & Company on the cliff edge side of the road.

As the train approached on that winter evening, a 30 ft section of the wall collapsed, together with 120 tons of soil and rock, and cascaded down on to the line. The train had just shut off steam on reaching the top of the 1 in 66 bank from Llwyngwril but was hit by the landslide in the darkness. The engine, No. 29 *Pegasus*, and its tender plunged down the cliff face killing the driver, William Davies, and his fireman of the same name. The first two coaches followed the locomotive over the edge, but miraculously the couplings held between these two and the third coach and guard's van, which remained on the line, holding the other two at a precarious angle. Only one passenger suffered from shock. Most of them, including Captain R. D. Pryce, a Cambrian director, were in the third coach.

The Board of Trade inspector, Colonel Rich, said in his report on the accident:

The only way of securing the railway from such accidents would be to tunnel through the mountain, which would be very expensive; had Parliament not sanctioned the making of the line round the headland it is probable that it never would have been made at all, as the traffic is small, does not meet the cost of the railway in its present form, and would do so in a less degree if more capital had been expanded.

Colonel Rich thought that the landslide was due to the excessively wet state of the peaty loam on the mountainside. He found that no blame attached to the Cambrian. There had been no slips for the previous two years, the line was regularly inspected and the speed limit strictly adhered to. He concluded that the road above should

K

be better drained and better maintained, the line carefully watched and the speed limit strictly observed.

The engine was later hauled back up the cliff and taken to Oswestry Works, where it was found to be repairable. It went on to run for another thirty years.

Acting on the inspector's recommendations, a permanent watchman was positioned at the cliffs. Two thousand pounds was also spent on improving the cliff face above the line, yet there was again a serious accident at Friog—but that lay many years ahead, in the GWR days of 1933.

Storms caused a lot of trouble on many exposed parts of the coast line—particularly in the early years when sea defences were crude and primitive. The most vicious storms often blew in January and that in 1877 caused £3,328 worth of damage, sweeping away four miles of track near Ynyslas. A year later the repair bill was only £11 less.

In the following year the Cambrian actually benefited from a storm—one which washed away the Llandulas viaduct on the LNWR North Wales main line on 29 August 1879. Ten trains each way were diverted via Afon Wen and Dolgelley. Altogether some 4,000 wagons were hauled over this route but the Cambrian had to offset a little of its windfall by paying the LNWR £150 for the hire of extra locomotives which it needed to handle diverted trains.

The storm of 1 January 1883 which caused the Friog accident brought a repair bill of just under £2,000. Being near the sea, the coast line usually escapes heavy snow, although Talerddig and the Mid Wales line suffered from time to time from snow blocks. Heavy falls blocked the coast for a time on 1 March 1886. A mixed train was trapped by drifts at Towyn and another bound for Pwllheli got stuck in drifts 8 ft to 10 ft deep at Friog.

TICKETS AND FARES

First class passengers were charged 2d to 2¼d a mile; second class at 1½d a mile and third class at the Parliamentary rate of 1d a mile. Ordinary returns were twice the single fare, but there were many returns designed to encourage certain types of traffic. Market returns were generally about one and a half times the single fare while special excursions offered returns which were considerably less than single fares. An 1864 excursion advertised 6s first and 3s second for a 126-mile round trip from Llanymynech to Borth. In periods when trade depression hung over Wales and traffic was slack, the Cambrian often introduced excursion and other special tickets to entice travellers. In July 1866 when the board felt the line was not carrying enough tourists, the traffic manager was asked to investigate the introduction of a through tourist ticket between Euston and the coast.

The special fares were rather below the cost of ordinary through return bookings which, in 1870, were:

	Aberystwyth		Barmouth	
	1st Class	2nd Class	1st Class	2nd Class
London	70s	53s	70s	53s
Shrewsbury	29s 6d	21s 6d	24s	17s
Manchester	38s	27s	32s 6d	23s
Liverpool	31s	22s	27s 6d	19s 6d
Cardiff	43s 6d	30s 6d	43s 6d	30s 6d

From 1 July 1881 first and second class fares were cut slightly. Privilege tickets for police and others cost $\frac{3}{4}$d a mile.

But not everyone was prepared to pay the correct fare—or even any fare at all. A shareholder complained in 1884 of getting into a first class compartment and finding it filled with fifteen or sixteen ladies with their butter baskets. 'Such a thing annoyed other ladies very much,' he lamented.

A fare dodge reported two years later was being used by people travelling north from Barmouth to Portmadoc. If they knew that tickets of Portmadoc passengers were collected when trains stopped at Minffordd, they simply said that they were going on to Carnarvon —and then walked off at Portmadoc unchallenged!

The repealing of the Cheap Trains Act on 1 October 1883, which abolished passenger duty on fares up to a penny a mile, saved the Cambrian about £100 a year. But the Cambrian did not benefit as much from it as some other companies as it had never added the duty to its passenger fares—a concession for which, the chairman told shareholders, it never got much gratitude.

By the eighties, the number of second class compartments provided on Cambrian trains had been greatly reduced, and on some branch trains, such as those to Kerry and Llanfyllin, only first and third class passengers were carried, despite the timetable showing all three classes on these trains. Quite what a second class traveller with a through booking did when changing at Abermule or Llanymynech is not known, but second class travel was definitely not encouraged—and it was to be abolished on the main line, as well as all branches, only a few years later. In the meantime, many second class coaches were downgraded to thirds.

K*

CHAPTER 10

Locomotives and Rolling Stock

EARLY LOCOMOTIVES: 1859-1866

Although the earliest engines were only named, numbers seem to have been added by the middle of 1864. There were several blanks in the numerical list and the missing numbers appear to have been allocated to Savin's own or Brecon & Merthyr locomotives. The oldest known list, of October 1861, shows seven engines belonging to the O & N, of which the first four were originally built for the L & N. The first, *Milford*, was an 0—4—2 saddle tank with 4 ft 9 in coupled wheels, 14 in x 20 in cylinders, and a heating surface of 660 sq ft. The others, the 'Volunteer' class, were 0—4—2 tender engines with 5 ft 0 in wheels, 15½ in x 22 in cylinders and 873 sq ft of heating surface. All were built by Sharp, Stewart & Company in 1859-60 and named:

3	*Milford*	7	*Llanerchydol*
4	*Wynnstay*	8	*Leighton*
5	*Montgomery*	9	*Volunteer*
6	*Glansevern*		

Nos. 4, 6, 7 and 8 were named after the homes of directors; No. 9 after the Montgomeryshire Railway Volunteers, a forerunner of the Territorials.

Late in 1861 Sharp, Stewart & Company supplied to the O & N two 0—6—0 goods engines, followed by two more in 1862 and four in 1863:

11	*Queen*	26	*Tubal Cain*
12	*Prince of Wales*	27	*Cambria*
19	*Hercules*	39	*Sir Watkin*
20	*Vulcan*	40	*Cyfronydd*

No. 39 was named after a director, Sir Watkin Williams-Wynn, and No. 40 after a director's residence. Known as the 'Queen' class, these engines had 4 ft 6 in wheels, 16 in x 24 in cylinders, 3 ft 11 in boilers and 952 sq ft of heating surface. Two more were taken over from the N & M in May 1863 when the working of that line was transferred to the O & N:

34	*Talerddig*	35	*Countess Vane*

No. 35 was renamed *Castell Deudraeth* (another director's home) early in 1866 and its former name transferred to No. 34. In 1867, No. 34 exchanged names with another engine, *Cader Idris*.

Also in 1863, 2—4—0 passenger engines were bought from the same makers. These had 5 ft 6 in wheels, 16 in x 20 in cylinders, 3 ft 10 in boilers and a heating surface of 843 sq ft.

28	*Mazeppa*	30	*Albion*
29	*Pegasus*	31	*Minerva*

Sharp, Stewart & Company built three 0—4—0 saddle tanks for the Porthywaen and Kerry branches in 1863:

36	*Plasfynnon*	38	*Prometheus*
37	*Mountaineer*		

Leading dimensions included 4 ft 0 in wheels, 14 in x 20 in cylinders and 669 sq ft of heating surface. No. 36 was named after another director's house.

At the end of 1863 the O & N Joint Committee took over eight small contractors' locomotives from Savin & Company, being used in the construction of lines. The oldest, No. 1 *Enterprise*, had been supplied originally to Davies and Savin by E. B. Wilson & Company in 1859 and was an 0—6—0 side tank with 3 ft 0 in wheels and cylinders 11 in by 18 in. No. 2 *Ruthin* was an 0—4—0 tender engine built by Manning Wardle & Company in 1860 and had 4 ft 0 in wheels, outside cylinders 14 in x 18 in. Most of the remaining engines were 0—6—0 saddle tanks of Manning's ubiquitous 'K' class. Savin bought eight but only five became Cambrian stock:

13	*Whixall*	18	*Cardigan*
14	*Nantclwyd*	24	*Borth*
17	*Merion*		

These engines were supplied in 1862-3 but No. 13 had been renamed *Green Dragon* by 1864. Cylinders were 12 in x 17 in and wheels 3 ft 1½ in. The other 'ballast' engine, as these were classified, was an 0—4—0 saddle tank built in 1862 by the Lilleshall Iron Company and shown at the London exhibition of that year. It was purchased by Savin in December and became No. 21 *Lilleshall*. It had outside cylinders 13 in x 20 in and 3 ft 0 in wheels.

The O & N obtained four more 'Albion' class 2—4—0s from Sharps in 1864:

41	*Cader Idris*	43	*Plynlimon*
42	*Glandovey*	44	*Rheidol*

No. 41 exchanged names with 0—6—0 No. 34 *Countess Vane* in 1867. These, then, were the engines which formed the initial stock of the Cambrian on its formation. The first engines purchased by the new company were four more 'Queen' class 0—6—0s and six 'Albions' from Sharps in 1864-5. The 0—6—0s were:

45	*Rhiewport*	51	*Snowdon*
46	*Towyn*	52	*Harlech*

No. 45 was yet another director's house. The 2—4—0 passenger engines were:

47	*Usk*	54	*Palmerston*
48	*Wye*	55	*Treflach*
53	*Gladstone*	56	*Whittington*

In 1865 the Cambrian ordered six 0—6—0 goods engines from Mannings and six 2—4—0 side tanks from Sharps, but due to the financial crisis following Savin's crash only three tanks were delivered; the other three tanks had not been started by the builders, but all the goods engines were completed and were sold instead to the London, Brighton & South Coast and Taff Vale Railways. The Cambrian numbers and names would have been:

57	*Aberystwyth*	To LB & SC	No. 219	in March 1866
58	*Barmouth*	,,	No. 220	,,
59	*Dolgelly*	To TVR	No. 66	in May 1866
60	*Carnarvon*	,,	No. 67	,,
61	*Aberdovey*	,,	No. 68	,,
62	*Portmadoc*	,,	No. 69	,,

The maker's numbers were 185 to 190. They had 16 in x 22 in cylinders and 4 ft 6 in wheels.

Presumably the 2—4—0 tanks would have been numbered 63 to 68. Those delivered in 1866 became:

57	*Maglona*	59	*Seaham*
58	*Gladys*		

No. 57 was named after the Roman Camp at Machynlleth; No. 58 after Earl Vane's daughter and No. 59 after his son, Lord Seaham. The engines had 4 ft 6 in coupled wheels, 14 in x 20 in cylinders, 3 ft 8 in boilers and a heating surface of 781 sq ft. They were the first Cambrian engines to have cabs, although rather primitive being simply a roof bent over to enclose the bunker. There were no side sheets.

WALKER'S LOCOMOTIVES : 1866-79

The forty-nine engines mentioned so far formed the Cambrian's stock when it took over the working of its own line after Savin's failure on 5 February 1866. Alexander Walker, who had been looking after the locomotives for Savin, was officially appointed locomotive superintendent the following April—not that he was able to superintend the forty-nine engines! No less than eleven were working on the Brecon & Merthyr and Hereford, Hay & Brecon railways, to which they had been transferred by Savin. The Brecon & Merthyr was allowed to retain five—Nos. 4, 6, 20, 47 and 48—but the remainder—Nos. 5, 8, 13, 19, 37 and 40—were eventually returned to the Cambrian. In addition, engine No. 9 was working on the Carnarvonshire Railway and No. 7 on the Denbigh, Ruthin & Corwen. Both were returned.

Blank numbers in the Cambrian list of 1866 were 10, 15, 16, 22, 23, 25, 32, 33, 49 and 50. To these could be added the numbers 4, 6, 20, 47, 48 (the five transferred to the B & M in 1865) and numbers 1, 13, 14, 17, 18, 21 and 24. These were 'ballast' engines withdrawn or sold between 1867-75. No. 1 *Enterprise* was advertised for sale with most of the others in April 1868. It failed to find a buyer and was converted to stationary use after being withdrawn in 1872. It was scrapped in 1894. The others were sold to industrial concerns. *Nantclwyd* later went to the LSWR as No. 458 *Jumbo*. The other 'ballast' engine, the 0—4—0 No. 2, had lost its name by 1864 and, although not withdrawn until 1886, rusted away at the back of Oswestry Works for several years. It was finally scrapped in 1896.

New locomotives obtained down to 1891 filled the blanks. All came from Sharps and the first four were 'Queen' class 0—6—0s :

1	*Victoria*	6	*Marquis*
4	*Alexandra*	10	*Marchioness*

The engines were built in 1872-3 and had six-wheel tenders, not apparently the first on the Cambrian as Nos. 45, 46, 51 and 52 had them at an early date and may have been built with them. The fitting of six-wheel tenders, later exchanged with several others of the 'Queen' class, depended on whether the locomotives were being used on the main line. Only one was fitted to the 2—4—0s, two or three having turns with it. An 0—6—0 side tank was the next engine, rather similar to the 'Queens' but with a larger boiler of 4 ft 2 in diameter, giving a heating surface of 1,041 sq ft. It had 17 in x 24 in cylinders. The wheels were 4 ft 6 in and the engine, delivered in 1875, became No. 13 *Talerddig*, as it had been ordered specially for banking. It had the same type of cab as the 'Seahams'.

At the end of 1875 the Cambrian locomotive stock stood at forty-two engines, all but one being of Sharp, Stewart & Company's design and build. The exception was the Manning, Wardle ballast engine No. 2. The most numerous class was the 'Queen' of seventeen 0—6—0 goods engines, followed by twelve 'Albion' 2—4—0 passenger type and four 'Volunteer' 0—4—2 mixed class. The other eight engines were all tanks, split into four classes: three 'Seaham' 2—4—0s; three 'Plasfynnon' 0—4—0STs; and two odd engines, No. 3 *Milford*, an 0—4—2ST, and the banker *Talerddig*.

Characteristically, the seven Sharp, Stewart classes bore a strong family likeness, having the maker's shapely chimney with wide, flared top, reputedly designed by Charles Beyer, and raised round-top fireboxes separated from the boilers by a broad polished brass band. Apart from the saddle tanks, the engines had shapely brass casings over the lock-up safety valves. (The 'Albions' were on a raised brass seating.) The 'Milford' and 'Plasfynnon' classes had short tanks not covering the raised fireboxes. These were surmounted by the dome with the safety valve on top. The others had Sharp's typical domes on the middle of the boiler barrel.

Only hand brakes with wooden brake blocks were fitted and tender engines had brakes only on tender wheels. Apart from the 'Albions', the springs were carried above the running plate. Those for the coupled wheels were behind the splashers; those for the rear wheels were inside the cab. All tender springs were above the running platforms, requiring narrow bodies typical of the period. On the 'Albions' only, the coupled wheels had springs below the axles.

The Sharp classes had rectangular brass nameplates fitted either to the centre or forward position on tanks or boiler barrels since the position of boiler feed-water clack boxes on the barrel varied, as did the shape of delivery pipes. All locomotives had Gifford injectors.

Polished brass beading distinguished the splashers of the 'Volunteer' and 'Albion' classes. The 'Albions' also had decorative open splashers, and with the 'Seahams' they also had small splashers for the leading wheels below the running plate. The 'Volunteers' originally had painted names on the cab side sheets, hence the below-centre position of the maker's plates. The various ballast tanks also had painted names. No. 1 *Enterprise* and the Manning, Wardle engines all had fluted safety valve castings and No. 2 *Ruthin* had a fluted dome as well. The others were domeless with short, flat-sided saddle tanks which, like *Lilleshall*, did not cover the smokebox or firebox. The latter had a dome over its raised firebox with the safety valves on top, the saddle tank being curved.

All engines had the meagre protection of only weatherboards over rectangular low cab side panels. The 'Seahams' had flared tops to the side tanks.

In the early days engines were dark green with triple lining of black and gold indented at panel corners, and red wheels. The only sign of ownership was a small rectangular brass plate fixed to the footplate angle above the driving axle. The same plates showed the engine number, there being no separate number plate. The plates, which made identification impossible except from a close side view, survived until 1909.

However, a few engines, including Nos. 3 and 45, had the same information in separate brass letters on the driving wheel splashers, the name of the railway being depicted 'CAMBRIAN RAILY COMPY'.

By 1878 the need for a larger engine than the little 'Albions', which weighed less than 25 tons, to work the principal main-line passenger trains was becoming acute. The result was that two 4—4—0s were introduced at a time when the type was unusual in Britain.

Besides bringing greatly increased power to the line, they also heralded a new look for Cambrian engines. For the first time they had proper cabs, Ramsbottom safety valves without a fancy casing, and neat built-up chimneys instead of Sharps old bell-mouth pattern. They had six-wheel tenders, although the only means of braking was still a tender hand-brake. Named in honour of the prime minister and the leader of the opposition, by means of separate brass letters on the leading splashers, these handsome engines were:

16 *Beaconsfield* 17 *Hartington*

The boiler was the same as *Talerddig*'s, but the pressure was increased to 140 lb—an advance of 20 lb pressure on all previous Cambrian engines. Cylinders were 17 in x 24 in and coupled wheels

5 ft 6½ in and the weight without tender was 33 tons 3 cwt. They cost £1,995 each.

In 1873-5 part of an order for 0—6—0 goods engines generally similar to the 'Queens' was built by Sharps for the Furness Railway but never delivered and sold to other railways instead. Two went to the MWR and one to the Denbigh, Ruthin & Corwen. Others remained unsold and in 1878—three years after they were built—the Cambrian bought two for £1,765 each and numbered them 14 and 15. In the meantime, the DR & C had been acquired by the LNWR and with it the Sharp's 0—6—0. This became LNWR No. 2346 and was sold to the Cambrian under duplicate No. 1881 the following year for £1,125. This compares with the cost price of the 1861 engines of £2,445. It became Cambrian No. 18 and all three were named after directors' homes:

14	*Broneirion*	18	*Orleton*
15	*Glansevern*		

Broneirion was David Davies' home on a hill overlooking the L & N at Llandinam. The engines had six-wheel tenders and were similar to the earlier 'Queens' except for the deep footplate angle at the front end.

ASTON'S LOCOMOTIVES: 1879-88

From about 1884 names were removed from *tender* engines as the directors felt named engines were ostentatious—although it was commonly supposed to be because English staff could not pronounce some of them! All names were removed by 1892, although only Nos. 3 and 13 of the tank engines had lost theirs, but the first unnamed engines had gone into service earlier. They were two more 4—4—0s of the 'Beaconsfield' class, delivered in 1886 and numbered 20 and 21. They were the last engines built for the Cambrian by Sharp's at their Atlas Works, Manchester, which closed in 1888. Subsequent engines were built at the former Clyde Locomotive Works at Glasgow, renamed Atlas Works by the firm. Nos. 20 and 21 were also the Cambrian's first engines to have vacuum ejectors for working the new continuous brakes and steam brakes for the engine. Their cost of £2,000 each was loaned by one of the directors, Arthur Buckley. They also differed from earlier locomotives of the class by having more prominent bogie wheel splashers than the slim type on Nos. 16 and 17. By about 1890, the first two engines of the class had been fitted with the later-type splasher.

The engines of the Mid Wales Railway were taken into Cambrian stock in April 1888. Originally, the company had twelve engines built by Kitson & Company of Leeds in 1864-5. Nos. 1 to 6 were 0—4—2 passenger engines with 5 ft 0 in wheels and 16 in x 22 in cylinders. Nos. 7 to 12 were 0—6—0 goods with 4 ft 6 in wheels and 16 in x 24 in cylinders. Both classes had the same boilers— 3 ft 9 in, with 903 sq ft of heating surface.

In July 1866, Nos. 2, 6 and 10 were sold to the Manchester, Sheffield & Lincolnshire Railway for £5,000 and renumbered 268 to 270. No. 11 was sold at the same time to the Denbigh, Ruthin & Corwen as No. 3. Later, it became LNWR No. 2348. When the MWR renumbered some of the remaining engines in 1873, the numbers 9 and 10 were left free for two new engines from Sharp's. These were the two previously mentioned as having been built for the Furness Railway and being identical to the Cambrian's Nos. 14, 15 and 18. They became Cambrian Nos. 48 and 49 in 1888.

Of the passenger 0—4—2s, No. 2 retained the same number in the Cambrian list. The others, Mid Wales 1, 3, 4 after 1873, were given the Cambrian numbers 22-24. The Kitson 0—6—0s became Nos. 5-8 and Cambrian numbers 25, 32, 33 and 47 when taken over in 1888.

All the locomotives had four-wheel tenders. No. 1 sported a copper-capped chimney and was first named *James Watt*, whose family lived near the line. It had lost its name by 1880. The Kitson engines were painted green with red frames, lined in red and blue, but the two 1873 engines were plain black. All had oval cab side number plates and on joining the Cambrian were provided with new plates in the same style. This was of two concentric ovals with the words 'Cambrian Railways' between the two and the number in the centre.

The livery during Aston's reign and probably for many years before 1879 was 'invisible green', a greenish black as distinct from the blueish black of the LNWR, and it was lined out in grey bands edged with vermilion. Name plates and the new oval number plates had a red background. Engines were unlettered except for the number on the red buffer beams. They were in gold, shaded with black. A new emblem of a divided shield bearing half a rose (for England) and half a dragon (for Wales) was applied to the splashers of the new 4—4—0s and also the 2—4—0 'Albions' from about 1886. Nos. 16 and 17 had the emblem on the cab sides as their names were on the splashers until these were removed by 1891. From 1886 the appearance of the 'Albions' changed. Open splashers were filled in and proper cabs and new chimneys similar to the 'Beaconsfields' were fitted by Aston, as well as vacuum brakes. Nos. 16 and 17 and two of the 'Volunteers' also had vacuum equipment fitted while most of the older engines had new cabs. In some cases these were purely extra wooden side sheets without a roof. Three of the 'Volunteers' also got Aston chimneys.

With the take-over of the Mid Wales locomotives, the number of engines in stock rose to 58 in 1888. Passenger services were worked by the four 'Beaconsfield' 4—4—0s, the twelve 'Albions' and eight 0—4—2s: four 'Volunteers' and four Mid Wales Kitsons. There were now twenty-six goods engines of the 0—6—0 type: twenty-two 'Queens' and four Kitsons. There were also the eight tank engines and *Talerddig* had a 'Beaconsfield' boiler. A boiler of the same size but with revised tube arrangement and increased pressure was used to rebuild the 'Queens'. The first two entered Oswestry Works in 1888 but only No. 15 was completed before the end of the year. As well as the larger boiler it had the new cab, built-up chimney, encased Ramsbottom safety valves and a new pattern of oval number plate, the old rectangular strip having been abandoned. It was to be the precursor of many similar rebuilds which also encompassed the 'Albions' and 'Seahams', but these took place after 1888 and so fall into volume two.

PASSENGER ROLLING STOCK

When the Cambrian first consolidated its stock in 1867, ninety-four passenger coaches were in service. Similar to others of the period they were all four-wheeled, generally 25 ft long on a 13 ft wheelbase with wooden underframes and spoked wheels and weighed about 8 tons. They had come from two main builders: the Ashbury Railway Carriage & Iron Company of Manchester and (slightly smaller ones) from the Metropolitan Railway Carriage & Wagon Company of Birmingham, formerly Joseph Wright & Sons. Their characteristics were high-waist bodies, narrow doors with the usual droplights, small quarter lights and a horizontal moulded strip about halfway down the lower side panels. About half the coaches —forty-six in fact—were thirds, including eight with brake-ends. The rest were twenty-nine composites, sixteen seconds and only three all-firsts. The composites had two central first compartments flanked by single seconds at each end and partitions between them rose to the roof. The firsts were reasonably upholstered, but the seconds had seat boards covered only with black American cloth

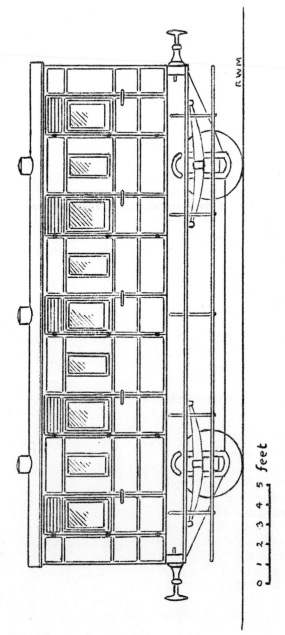

R.W.M.

0 1 2 3 4 5 feet

The type of third-class carriage built at Oswestry from 1866

which, though easy to clean, was extremely slippery for passengers. The thirds were spartan with only bare boards for seats and no partitions. The brake-thirds had three passenger compartments and double-glazed doors at one end.

Oswestry also built a number of coaches similar to the originals, but the thirds were even more primitive. Besides droplights in the doors of the five compartments, there were only four other small windows on each side. The composites looked more modern with lower waist-lines and bigger windows. They were also 25 ft long x 8 ft wide and closely resembled Richard Bore's LNWR four-wheelers of the sixties, having curved mouldings at the side panel ends, like road coaches. The first compartments remained central, flanked by seconds. Four-wheelers of the seventies and eighties had normal mouldings. They included some vehicles with the number of third compartments reduced from five to four, which gave a big increase in leg room, and several of these survived down to GWR days. Some composites accommodated all three classes.

Four-wheel passenger brakevans of the late sixties and early seventies matched the original coaches, having double-glazed doors at each end and a guard's look-out ducket, possibly added after construction.

The progression from four- to six-wheel coaches was gradual and although the first six-wheeler was built at Oswestry in 1870, the last four-wheeler was not completed until 1889. Besides being the first six-wheeled coach, a saloon built for the chairman at Oswestry in 1870 introduced Mansell wooden centre wheels to the Cambrian. The 27 ft 6 in body was divided into two saloons without end windows, separated by a servant's compartment and toilet. A roof water tank resembled a short length of clerestory. After a short time the saloon was repainted in Earl Vane's house colours of lilac and yellow and in 1892 it was transferred into ordinary service and later worked on the Llangynog branch.

Early six-wheel coaches were 28 ft long and of two main types: a five-compartment third and a composite of four compartments with double windowless luggage doors in the centre. First class compartments were now upholstered in blue broad cloth; above the luggage rack the partitions were covered in a drab rep, and the ceilings were panelled in sycamore. The seconds had striped plush upholstery and ceilings covered in American oilcloth. The thirds, well fitted out for the period, had seats covered with brown rep. The upper partitions and ceilings were finished in grained wood. Also of 28 ft length were a number of guards' brakevans with third-class accommodation. Some had two compartments at one end; others had an extra compartment at the other end. Both types had central look-out duckets which increased the width from 8 ft to 8 ft 10 in. The duckets, not quite as high as the coach sides, had flat tops for a lamp fitting.

In the earliest coaches oil lamps were withdrawn through the roof for lighting. First class compartments had their own lamps in glass globes, but adjacent thirds had to share a single lamp. The lamps were taken to trains in handcarts. They were lit on the platform and handed to a porter who walked along coach roofs, putting lamps through flaps into compartments. Oil lamps were still used in the improved six-wheeled carriages of the late eighties.

The livery of the original coaches was dark brown on lower side panels and ends with white upper sides and a black edged gold lining. They were repainted in the familiar green and white, probably in the late sixties. The lower side panels and ends were in bronze green and upper sides and waists in white. Mouldings were lined out in black, gold and red and the lettering was in gold shaded blue. Roofs were white; underframes, black.

Besides building new carriages at Oswestry, the company also placed orders with outside contractors, notably the Metropolitan Railway Carriage & Wagon Company of Birmingham, although they were limited by lack of money. To overcome one 'squeeze', one of the Cambrian's directors, Arthur Buckley, lent £15,411 for rolling stock purchased in 1885-7.

Nos.			Each
154-157	4	6w lavatory first coaches	£435
129-34/58-63	12	6w third class coaches	£260 - £298
126-8/49-53	8	6w composite coaches	£300 - £324
135-138	4	6w passenger brake vans	£233
139-145	7	4w horse boxes	£134
	30	4w cattle trucks	£63-£67

The absorption of the stock of the Mid Wales Railway in April 1888 brought an influx of coaches, mostly about 24 years old. Originally the MWR had fifty-eight coaches, all four-wheeled and similar to early Cambrian designs. They consisted of twenty-four third class, fourteen seconds, eight firsts, eight composites and four passenger brakevans. The fifty-eight cost £21,275, but they soon proved to be too many and in 1867 eight of the seconds, six thirds and three firsts were sold. In December 1888 another three coaches were sold to the Golden Valley Railway. The small number of

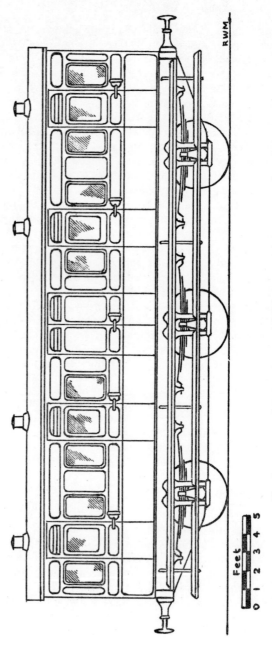

The latest type of composite coach with luggage compartment in 1888

Feet
0 1 2 3 4 5

passenger brakes suggests that long trains of eleven coaches or so were expected to be a regular make-up.

It was a wild dream because from the start the Mid Wales was embarrassed by a surplus of every type of rolling stock. Not only did coaches deteriorate through standing idle for long periods, but they also suffered from having to stand out in the open exposed to all weathers. The first carriage shed was not finished until autumn 1867. It was built at Rhayader and all it could hold was twelve coaches, one-fifth of the stock, which had a brick red livery.

GOODS ROLLING STOCK

The original stock of about 1,000 wagons differed little from contemporary designs of other companies. Open wagons were mostly low-sided with dumb buffers—wooden solebars which extended beyond the ends to form solid buffers. Many wagons had no brakes while those which were fitted normally had them on one side only. Bodies were similar to wooden types built down to nationalisation.

Early high-sided wagons had only four or five plank sides with a depth of about 3 ft. Low-sided wagons had two or three planks and some had sides which could be dropped. Wheelbases were generally 9 ft to 9 ft 6 in and lengths were about 15 ft 6 in. Van heights were low at about 10 ft 6 in. In contrast to the 'modern' appearance of wagons, older covered vans looked rather archaic, their bodies having stout outside frames and bracing and double-hinged instead of sliding doors.

Due to the acute shortage of money there were few additions to the original fleet for several years and the first big order was not placed until 1877. It went to the North of England Wagon Company of Hartlepool and it was for 115 wagons with spring buffers, each costing £57 17s 6d. Oswestry was now busy building new stock, including brakevans, and thirty cattle trucks bought in 1886 brought goods stock up to the 1,500 mark. Two years later the absorption of the MWR resulted in a major influx of stock. The MWR originally had two hundred low-sided and one hundred and fifty high-sided open wagons, fifty each of lime trucks and goods vans, forty cattle and thirty timber trucks and six goods brakes—426 which cost £49,392. As with the passenger stock, the MWR soon found it had more wagons than it needed and it disposed of one hundred and thirteen wagons—including fifty to the Manchester, Sheffield & Lincolnshire Railway in 1866 for £2,500. Many of the lime trucks were converted into coal wagons at a cost of £8 each.

But there was one type of wagon which the MWR originally under-ordered. Its area was heavily afforested and landowners quickly began using the line to get timber to rapidly-growing towns and cities. Not only was it cheaper to send timber by rail, but far quicker at a time when horses took days to trundle along narrow, hilly roads. To meet the shortage of timber trucks, the MWR bought another twenty-five in 1873.

Altogether, the Cambrian received 338 goods vehicles from the MWR in 1888. MWR wagons were repaired at Builth Wells and also at Thomas's Wagon Works at Llanidloes. In the early days there were many complaints of damage to wagons working over the Brecon & Merthyr caused by its use of spragging (inserting bars between the spokes) on its steep inclines. The MWR complained to the B & M that it was not using brakevans of sufficient weight and power.

The goods livery was a medium-light grey with ironwork and strapping in black and solebars grey. Wagon numbers were painted on the ends in white. There was no lettering on wagon sides in those days, ownership being denoted by an oval number plate on the solebars. In some cases the Cambrian's title was given in the singular!

Total carriage stock rose from 125 in 1884 to 163 by 1888, including 38 six-wheel vehicles built from 1885. Most survived to grouping, the last being withdrawn in 1930. In contrast, only 13 four-wheel vehicles went into GWR service and all had been scrapped by 1925.

Most MWR coaches were given Cambrian numbers between 164 and 199, but few survived after 1895. New six-wheel coaches added to stock in 1888 included post office sorting van No. 200, a 32 ft 0 in vehicle with off-centre gangway connections. Then the longest Cambrian coach, it lasted until 1924, finally becoming GWR No. 810.

From the mid-eighties the Cambrian settled down to a period of slow and steady, if unspectacular, consolidation. Trade—and train services—were improving and summer travel was getting more popular. Things might have continued in that peaceful vein without any serious disturbance but for an accident at Ellesmere at 3 o'clock in the morning of 6 November 1887, when the down mail was derailed at facing points. No one was hurt and the incident was minor. Yet the consequences of it were to rumble for years and shake—although not break—the Cambrian management.

The train had been switched to the wrong line and was derailed on a length of poor track. Conacher ordered it to be replaced before the arrival on the scene, several days later, of the Board of Trade Inspector, Colonel Rich. Because this was done, he found nothing to criticise in his report about the track. But he was critical that the only man at the station—a porter named Humphreys—had then been on duty for nineteen hours. It was found that he reached the ground frame too late to correctly set the road as the mail ran into the station under clear signals. Humphreys claimed his long spell of duty had caused his vigilance to be affected. The Cambrian management, which held its own inquiry, found otherwise. It said that Humphreys had time to play cards while waiting for the mail and dismissed him. The stationmaster was also posted away for not making better staff arrangements. But he was a man who was now to prove not only his integrity, but also his personal courage. His name, which became known throughout the whole of Britain to the Cambrian's embarrassment, was John Hood.

His integrity had been acknowledged already by others during the twenty-two years he had been with the Cambrian, which he joined as a clerk at Llanymynech in 1869. For all but two of those years, he was a stationmaster. For four and a half years before moving to Ellesmere, he was at Criccieth and local people there thought so much of him that as a farewell they presented him with a testimonial and a purse of gold.

Hood did not rest content at the injustice to Humphreys and stated in public that the real cause of the Ellesmere accident was the rotten track. He also signed a petition asking for the porter's reinstatement. The board was furious, feeling that a man in Hood's position should support the management, not the men. Conacher, as general manager, suspended Hood for fourteen days and then he was posted as stationmaster at Montgomery. As he moved once again, the people of Ellesmere paid warm tribute to his work and he received a presentation similar to the one made to him at Criccieth when he went to Montgomery early in 1888.

There the matter might have rested for ever, but for the growing political tensions of the day which included strong and growing agitation against long hours being worked by railwaymen, not only on the Cambrian, but throughout Britain. The Amalgamated Society of Railway Servants which, as the forerunner of the National Union of Railwaymen, had been formed in 1872, was also gaining strength. It had a lobby in Parliament which began to match that of the railway directors who represented over one-eighth of the members of the Commons and the Lords.

The Hood case, as it was to become known, got national prominence when a Select Committee was set up to inquire into the long hours of railwaymen. But that was not until 1891—and volume two —and so, for the moment, we must leave the matter, with Hood quietly and efficiently (for there was plenty of evidence of that) going about his duties as stationmaster at Montgomery.

Appendices

1 : AUTHORISATION AND OPENING DATES : 1853-1888

	Authorised		Opened		
LLANIDLOES & NEWTOWN RAILWAY					
Llanidloes - Newtown	4 Jun	1853	30 Apr	1859	(g)
			2 Sep	1859	(p)
OSWESTRY & NEWTOWN RAILWAY					
Oswestry - Pool Quay	26 Jun	1855	1 May	1860	
Pool Quay - Welshpool	26 Jun	1855	14 Aug	1860	
Abermule - Newtown	26 Jun	1855	14 Aug	1860	
Welshpool - Abermule	26 Jun	1855	10 Jun	1861	
Llynclys - Porthywaen	3 Jul	1860	1 May	1861	(g)
			5 Jan	1904	(p)
Abermule - Kerry	17 May	1861	2 Mar	1863	(g)
			1 Jul	1863	(p)
Llanymynech - Llanfyllin	17 May	1861	17 Jul	1863	
NEWTOWN & MACHYNLLETH RAILWAY					
Moat Lane to Machynlleth	27 Jul	1857	3 Jan	1863	
OSWESTRY, ELLESMERE & WHITCHURCH RAILWAY					
Ellesmere - Whitchurch	1 Aug	1861	20 Apr	1863	(g)
			4 May	1863	(p)
Oswestry - Ellesmere	1 Aug	1861	27 Jul	1864	
CAMBRIAN RAILWAYS					
Amalgamation of above four Railways	25 Jul	1864			
ABERYSTWYTH & WELSH COAST RAILWAY					
Machynlleth - Borth	22 Jul	1861	1 Jul	1863	
Aberdovey - Llwyngwril	22 Jul	1861	24 Oct	1863	
Borth - Aberystwyth	22 Jul	1861	23 Jun	1864	
Llwyngwril - Barmouth Junction	22 Jul	1861	3 Jul	1865	
Barmouth Junction - Penmaenpool	29 Jul	1862	3 Jul	1865	
Glandovey Junction - Aberdovey	5 Jul	1865	14 Aug	1867	
Barmouth Junction - Barmouth	22 Jul	1861	3 Jun	1867	(p)
			10 Oct	1867	(g)
Barmouth - Portmadoc	22 Jul	1861	10 Oct	1867	
Portmadoc - Pwllheli	29 Jul	1862	10 Oct	1867	
Penmaenpool - Dolgelley	29 Jul	1862	21 Jun	1869	(p)
			1 Oct	1869	(g)
Extension to Dolgelley GWR	29 Jul	1862	1 Aug	1869	
Absorbed by Cambrian Railways	5 Jul	1865			

	Authorised	Opened
MID WALES RAILWAY		
Llanidloes - Newbridge	1 Aug 1859	1 Sep 1864 (g)
		21 Sept 1864 (p)
Newbridge - Three Cocks	3 Jul 1860	1 Sep 1864 (g)
		21 Sep 1864 (p)
Three Cocks - Talyllyn	3 Jul 1860	1 Sep 1864 (g)
		19 Sep 1864 (p)
Builth Road curve to LNWR	30 Jun 1864	1 Nov 1866
Worked by Cambrian Railways from	2 Apr 1888	
POTTERIES, SHREWSBURY & NORTH WALES RAILWAY		
Llanymynech - Nantmawr	7 May 1862	13 Aug 1866 (g)
		18 Apr 1870 (p)
Worked by Cambrian Railways from	1 Jun 1881	

(g) Opened for goods traffic
(p) Opened for passenger traffic

2 : MILEAGE OWNED AND WORKED : 1888

Lines owned				Miles	Chains
Whitchurch - Aberystwyth	..	...	...	96	32
Glandovey Junction - Pwllheli	...	...	...	54	12
Llynclys Junction - Porthywaen	...	...	...	1	65
Llanymynech - Llanfyllin	..	...	...	9	13
Abermule - Kerry	...	...	...	3	55
Moat Lane - Llanidloes	...	...	...	7	50
Barmouth Junction - Dolgelley	..	...	...	7	36
				180	33
Lines worked					
Llanymynech - Nantmawr	...	...	...	3	75
Llanidloes - Talyllyn .	...	...	...	48	64
				52	59
		Add lines owned		180	33
				233	12

3: CHIEF OFFICERS: 1888

CAMBRIAN RAILWAYS

Chairman	James F. Buckley
Secretary	John Conacher
Engineer	George Owen
Passenger superintendent	F. Vaughan
Goods superintendent	J. Shepherd
Locomotive superintendent	William Aston
Stores superintendent	T. S. Goldsworthy
Accountant	Richard Brayne
Audit clerk	William Finchett
Solicitor	Hy. Christian Corfield

MID WALES RAILWAY

Chairman	Samuel Gurney Sheppard
Secretary	John Wade
General Manager	Frank Grundy
Engineer and locomotive superintendent	G. F. Ellis
Solicitor	S. F. Noyes

4: CAMBRIAN RAILWAYS LOCOMOTIVES: 1859-88

No.	Name	Type	Built		Maker's No.	Remarks
1	Enterprise	0—6—0T	Mar	1859	EBW 601	Wdn 1872, scr 1894
1	Victoria	0—6—0	Jun	1872	SS 2231	
2	Ruthin	0—4—0	Oct	1860	MW 19	Wdn 1886, scr 1896
3	Milford	0—4—2ST	Mar	1859	SS 1123	
4	Wynnstay	0—4—2	Oct	1859	SS 1146	To B & M 1865, scr 18
4	Alexandra	0—6—0	Jun	1872	SS 2232	
5	Montgomery	0—4—2	Oct	1859	SS 1147	
6	Glansevern	0—4—2	Nov	1859	SS 1148	To B & M 1865, scr 18
6	Marquis	0—6—0	Jul	1873	SS 2306	
7	Llanerchydol	0—4—2	Dec	1860	SS 1224	
8	Leighton	0—4—2	Dec	1860	SS 1225	
9	Volunteer	0—4—2	Dec	1860	SS 1226	
10	Marchioness	0—6—0	Aug	1873	SS 2307	
11	Queen	0—6—0	Dec	1861	SS 1301	
12	Prince of Wales	0—6—0	Dec	1861	SS 1302	
13	Whixall	0—6—0ST	Jan	1862	MW 36	Rn Green Dragon b 1864. Sold Oct 1868
13	Talerddig	0—6—0T	Feb	1875	SS 2452	
14	Nantclwyd	0—6—0ST	Apr	1862	MW 45	Sold Aug 1868
14	Broneirion	0—6—0	Sep	1875	SS 2511 ⎱	New from makers
15	Glansevern	0—6—0	Sep	1875	SS 2513 ⎰	Mar 1878
16	Beaconsfield	4—4—0	Aug	1878	SS 2789	
17	Merion	0—6—0ST	Aug	1862	MW 52	Sold 1875
17	Hartington	4—4—0	Aug	1878	SS 2790	
18	Cardigan	0—6—0ST	Oct	1862	MW 55	Sold 1874
18	Orleton	0—6—0	Sep	1875	SS 2510	Ex-LNWR No. 1881 Dec 1879
19	Hercules	0—6—0	Nov	1862	SS 1341	
20	Vulcan	0—6—0	Nov	1862	SS 1342	To B & M 1865, scr 1
20	—	4—4—0	Jul	1886	SS 3356	
21	Lilleshall	0—4—0ST		1862	LI	New from makers Dec 1862. Sold 186
21	—	4—4—0	Jul	1886	SS 3357	
24	Borth	0—6—0ST	Jan	1863	MW 66	Sold Dec 1867
26	Tubal Cain	0—6—0	Feb	1863	SS 1343	
27	Cambria	0—6—0	Feb	1863	SS 1344	
28	Mazeppa	2—4—0	Mar	1863	SS 1400	
29	Pegasus	2—4—0	Mar	1863	SS 1401	
30	Albion	2—4—0	Mar	1863	SS 1412	
31	Minerva	2—4—0	Mar	1863	SS 1413	
34	Talerddig	0—6—0	Dec	1861	SS 1310	Rn Countess Vane 1866 Cader Idris in 1867
35	Countess Vane	0—6—0	Dec	1861	SS 1311	Rn Castell Deudra in 1866
36	Plasfynnon	0—4—0ST	Jun	1863	SS 1431	
37	Mountaineer	0—4—0ST	Jun	1863	SS 1432	
38	Prometheus	0—4—0ST	Jun	1863	SS 1433	

Name	Type	Built		Maker's No.	Remarks
Sir Watkin	0—6—0	Jul	1863	SS 1445	
Cyfronydd	0—6—0	Jul	1863	SS 1446	
Cader Idris	2—4—0	Mar	1864	SS 1485	Rn *Countess Vane* in 1867
Glandovey	2—4—0	Mar	1864	SS 1486	
Plynlimon	2—4—0	Mar	1864	SS 1487	
Rheidol	2—4—0	Mar	1864	SS 1488	
Rhiewport	0—6—0	Aug	1864	SS 1530	
Towyn	0—6—0	Aug	1864	SS 1531	
Usk	2—4—0	Apr	1865	SS 1579	To B & M Oct 1865, scr 1887
Wye	2—4—0	Apr	1865	SS 1580	To B & M Oct 1865, scr 1904
Snowdon	0—6—0	Apr	1865	SS 1590	
Harlech	0—6—0	May	1865	SS 1597	
Gladstone	2—4—0	Oct	1865	SS 1633	
Palmerston	2—4—0	Oct	1865	SS 1632	
Treflach	2—4—0	Dec	1865	SS 1655	
Whittington	2—4—0	Dec	1865	SS 1656	
Maglona	2—4—0T	May	1866	SS 1681	
Gladys	2—4—0T	May	1866	SS 1682	
Seaham	2—4—0T	May	1866	SS 1683	

Abbreviations:

B & M	Brecon & Merthyr Railway
EBW	E. B. Wilson & Company, Leeds
LI	Lilleshall Iron Company, Oakengates
LNWR	London & North Western Railway
MW	Manning, Wardle & Company, Leeds
Rn	Renamed
Scr	Scrapped
SS	Sharp, Stewart & Company, Manchester
ST	Saddle tank
T	Side tank
Wdn	Withdrawn

5: MID WALES RAILWAY LOCOMOTIVES: 1864-88

1864 No.	1873 No.	Name	Type	Built		Maker's No.		Remarks
1	1	*James Watt*	0—4—2	Nov	1864	K	1235	Cam No. 22
2	—	—	0—4—2	Nov	1864	K	1236	To MS & L Jul 1
3	2	—	0—4—2	Nov	1864	K	1237	Cam No. 2
4	4	—	0—4—2	Nov	1864	K	1238	Cam No. 24
5	3	—	0—4—2	Dec	1864	K	1239	Cam No. 23
6	—	—	0—4—2	Mar	1865	K	1240	To MS & L Jul 1
7	7	—	0—6—0	May	1865	K	1247	Cam No. 33
8	8	—	0—6—0	May	1865	K	1248	Cam No. 47★
9	5	—	0—6—0	Jun	1865	K	1249	Cam No. 25
10	—	—	0—6—0	Oct	1865	K	1250	To MS & L Jul 1
11	—	—	0—6—0	Oct	1865	K	1251	To DR & C Jul 1
12	6	—	0—6—0	Oct	1865	K	1252	Cam No. 32
—	9	—	0—6—0	Oct	1873	SS	2339	Cam No. 48
—	10	—	0—6—0	Nov	1873	SS	2347	Cam No. 49

★ Cambrian No. not shown on this engine

Abbreviations:

Cam	Cambrian Railways, from Apr 1888
DR & C	Denbigh, Ruthin & Corwen Railway
K	Kitson & Co, Leeds
MS & L	Manchester, Sheffield & Lincolnshire Railway
SS	Sharp, Stewart & Co, Manchester

Acknowledgements

Our main source of reference has been the official records of the Cambrian Railways and its constituent companies kept in the British Transport Historical Records Office, London. While our research was being carried out, the rule forbidding access to official records under fifty years old was relaxed to cover the period to Grouping and this proved most useful. We are most grateful to the Archivist Mr E. Atkinson and his enthusiastic staff for their help and patience in tracking down information.

Highly valued help has been given by Messrs C. A. Appleton, Roger Morris, Bernard Roberts, Oliver Veltom and, in official circles, by Frank Allen, Public Relations Officer, London Midland Region, Liverpool, and the Region's Public Relations Department at Euston; Manchester and Lancashire Public Libraries, The National Library of Wales, the Railway Museum, York, and many men of the Cambrian and Great Western railways.

Other sources have been GWR records and Board of Trade Reports and Returns. Where an alternative opening date has been found, the one quoted has been selected in the light of evidence available.

Numerous books have been consulted, notably *The Story of the Cambrian* by C. P. Gasquoine, *Nineteenth Century Railway Carriages* by C. Hamilton Ellis, *Locomotives of the Great Western Railway* prepared by the Railway Correspondence & Travel Society, *Narrow Gauge Rails in Mid-Wales* and *Narrow Gauge Rails to Portmadoc* by J. I. C. Boyd, *The Brecon & Merythyr Railway* by D. S. M. Barrie, *The Wrexham, Mold & Connah's Quay Railway* by J. M. Dunn, *The Cambrian Railways* by R. W. Kidner, *The Railway Engineers* by O. S. Nock, and Bradshaw's *Railway Shareholders Guide*.

Other useful references have been various 'standard' railway histories including Steel's *London and North Western*, McDermot's *Great Western* and Dow's *Great Central*. For branch lines, mention must be made of the Lewis Cozens books on the Rheidol, Llanfair, Mawddwy, Llanfyllin, Van and Kerry branches, *The Vale of Rheidol Railway* by W. J. K. Davies and *The Hay Railway* by C. R. Clinker.

For economic and other information we have consulted a wide variety of books, notably Murray's *Handbook for Travellers in South Wales* (1860), *The Story of Montgomeryshire* by J. E. Roberts and Robert Owen (1916), *Wales, a Physical, Historical and Regional*

Geography edited by E. G. Bowen, *Brief Glory* by D. W. Morgan, *The Industrial Revolution in North Wales* by A. H. Dodd, *The Railwaymen* by Philip S. Bagwell and *Engines and Men* by J. B. Raynes, *The Golden Valley Railway* by C. L. Mowat.

For illustrations our special thanks are due to Messrs C. C. Green and Ben Jones. Plates 1, 2 and 3 were taken by H. W. Burman. Talerddig Cutting (Plate 7) is reproduced from *Top Sawyer*, Ivor Thomas' biography of David Davies, by kind permission of Longmans, Green & Company Limited. Other photographs are reproduced by courtesy of Locomotive & General Railway Photographs (Plates 5, 6, 10, 11, 12, 27, 32, 34. Of these, Plates 5 and 6 were by Dr T. F. Budden; the rest by F. E. Fox Davies); R. E. Bleasdale (Plates 13, 16, 19, 26); and British Railways (Plate 36). The remainder are from the collection of R. W. Miller. Park Pictures (Manchester) Limited improved many faded originals.

Text illustrations of notices and working timetables are reproduced by courtesy of British Transport Historical Records (pages 93, 130 and 131).

REX CHRISTIANSEN and

Whitefield, Manchester.   R. W. MILLER
January 1967

NOTE TO THE REVISED EDITION

A number of people were kind enough to write to us after the publication of the original volume. Some of their comments and notes have been included in this edition; others we are keeping for use in any revise of the second volume. We are especially grateful to R. I. Cartwright, C. R. Clinker, H. Forster, C. C. Green, M. D. Greville, J. Hargreaves, M. E. Morton Lloyd, J. Williams, the Historical Model Railway Society, the Railway & Canal Historical Society, the John Rylands Library, Manchester.

Extra Cambriana we have found additional to that listed in volume II, includes a Cambrian coat of arms on the station at Frankton; a Welsh Midland Railway share certificate of 1848 in the Railway Museum at York; a notice at Clapham announcing the 1869 opening of the section between Penmaenpool and Dolgelley.

Occasionally Cambrian hand-lamps, pocket watches and timetables are offered for sale by collectors or dealers. They realise keen prices, reflecting the esteem in which The Cambrian Railways is still held by people far too young to have ever known it in its hey-day.

REX CHRISTIANSEN and

Whitefield, Manchester.   R. W. MILLER
March 1971

Index

Illustrations are indicated by heavy type

Summer Tours in North Wales.

BATHING, BOATING, FISHING (Sea, River & Lake), COACHING, MOUNTAINEERING.

1st, 2nd, and 3rd Class Tourist Tickets,

Available for Two Calendar Months, renewable up to 31st December, are issued from 1st May to 31st October at all the principal Stations in England to **Aberystwith, Aberdovey, Towyn, Dolgelley, Barmouth, Criccieth, Borth, Harlech, Portmadoc, and Pwllheli.**

The Scenery traversed by and adjoining the Cambrian Railways is of an exceedingly varied and beautiful description, and the Coast of Cardigan Bay, to which the line affords the most convenient access, offers great advantages for sea-bathing in the long reaches of firm, safe, and sandy beach, with which it abounds, and in its pure and bracing air. The mountain ranges of SNOWDON, CADER IDRIS, and PLYNLIMON, with their Rivers and Lakes, are also readily accessible from the various Watering-places, thus placing within the reach of visitors a delightful combination of the natural beauties of sea and land.

Arrangements are made during the Summer Months for the conveyance of Visitors by Coach to and from places of interest in the vicinity of the Line at reduced charges, by which means, and also by the Festiniog, Talyllyn, and Corris miniature-gauge railways, whose termini are on the Cambrian system, the following amongst other places can easily be visited by daily Excursions :—

Snowdon, Beddgelert, Tan-y-bwlch, Festiniog Slate Quarries, Cwmbychan Lake, Mawddach Estuary, Precipice Walk and Torrent Walk (Dolgelley), Talyllyn Lake, Corris, Rheidol Lake, Devil's Bridge, &c.

Special Tickets at Reduced Fares

Are also issued between Local Stations to TOURISTS, and for FISHING, PIC-NIC and OTHER PARTIES.

A Special Service of Express Trains

Is run, daily during the season, in connection with Fast trains on the London and North Western and other Railways, with Through Carriages between the following Stations :—

London (Euston) and **Aberystwith** and **Barmouth**
Viâ Stafford, Shrewsbury, and Welshpool.

Stafford and **Barmouth**—Viâ Shrewsbury and Welshpool.

Hereford (Midland) and **Aberystwith**
Viâ Three Cocks, Rhayader, and Llanidloes.

Newport (B. & M.) and **Aberystwith**
Viâ Talyllyn, Builth, and Llanidloes.

Swansea and **Aberystwith**
Viâ Brecon, Builth, and Llanidloes.

Manchester (London Road) and **Aberystwith**
Viâ Crewe, Ellesmere, and Welshpool.

Liverpool (Lime Street) and **Aberystwith**
Viâ Crewe, Ellesmere, and Welshpool.

Through Carriages run daily throughout the year between London (Euston) and Aberystwith.

"PICTURESQUE WALES" (Illustrated).

The Official Guide Book to the Cambrian Railways, edited by Mr. GODFREY TURNER, price 6d., can be obtained at the Bookstalls, or on application to the Company's Offices or Stations.

Tourist Programmes and further particulars of Trains, Fares, &c., may be obtained at any of the Company's Stations or Booking Offices, or on application to the undersigned.

COMPANY'S OFFICE, OSWESTRY.   **J. CONACHER, Secretary.**

An 1885 advertisement in a guide to Scotland: The Cambrian's crusading zeal was noted by the LNWR Superintendent of the Line, G. P. Neele, who wrote in his *Railway Reminiscences* about when the line was opened from Machynlleth to Aberystwyth in 1864:

Mr Findlay, the Manager, was very urgent that we at Euston, by tourist announcements, maps, and through booking with coaching proprietors, should give all possible publicity to the completion of the line.